Encountering the love, faithfulness  chapter, has pulled my heart even c and mind have grown in love as I h. pathways and surprise healings, enjoying peaceful rest and delightful moments with Him. *Jesus and Me* is a book that will go on my shelf of books to read over and over again. ~ Sharon

This book captivated my heart and soul! As I turned each page diving deeper into Kimberly's personal story, a desire birthed within me to experience that same personal intimacy with Jesus that she so openly shares. Through her transparency and captivating writing, I am convinced that Jesus and Papa God genuinely care about every detail of our past, present, and future; yet most importantly, they care about our hearts. Her story, along with her explanations and exercises, offer an open invitation to a divine relationship and inner healing for anyone who desires such freedom and filling of peace and joy! ~ Katie

Kimberly's honesty and humility leap off the pages of this book. Her willingness to share her healing journey, alongside scripture, scientific insights, and easy-to-follow exercises in Part II, make it simple to begin one's own journey of healing with Jesus. This is a book for everyone—a book I will keep on hand at all times to give out to others who are struggling. There is hope and healing with Jesus in the Secret Place and within the pages of *Jesus and Me*. ~ Andy

Some people are placed on this earth to act as pioneers and to forge new trails. Their stories must be told. Kimberly is one of those pioneers with a story to be shared. In your hands, you hold a book of real stories interwoven with powerful, freedom-fighting steps. It is an invitation to encounter Jesus on a deeper level; to personally know Him as your Healer and Redeemer. While I am in the midst of my own healing journey, this book and the author have guided me on a path toward greater healing and freedom. The pages in front of you will give life to your journey of hope and healing, so take a deep breath, steady yourself, and step forth into the future that your Divine Creator has for you! ~ Kara

JESUS and Me

A JOURNEY OF LOVE, HEALING, AND FREEDOM

*Find Healing for Your Soul
from the Pain of Your Past*

KIMBERLY ANN WEBER

Debbie ~ You held a very special place in Father Gods heart. May His love permeate every area of your being as you journey thru "Jesus + Me" You are created by Love, to be loved, + to share this Love w/ others. Bless you! Nothing is wasted in His hands.

Kimberly ann

Kimberly Ann Weber

Sparkling Brooks Ministries

Contact: Kimberly@SparklingBrooks.com

ISBN 978-1-54394-923-0 eBook 978-1-54394-924-7

Copyright © 2019 Kimberly Ann Weber

For Worldwide Distribution. Printed in the United States of America

All Scripture quotations, unless otherwise indicated, are taken from the *Holy Bible, New International Version®*, NIV®. Copyright ©1973, 1978, 1984, 2011 by Biblica, Inc.™ Used by permission of Zondervan. All rights reserved worldwide. www.zondervan.com The "NIV" and "New International Version" are trademarks registered in the United States Patent and Trademark Office by Biblica, Inc.™

Scripture quotations marked (GNT) are from the *Good News Translation* in Today's English Version- Second Edition Copyright © 1992 by American Bible Society. Used by Permission.

Scripture taken from the *New King James Version®*. Copyright © 1982 by Thomas Nelson. Used by permission. All rights reserved.

Scripture quotations marked NLT are taken from the *Holy Bible, New Living Translation,* copyright © 1996, 2004, 2015 by Tyndale House Foundation. Used by permission of Tyndale House Publishers, Inc., Carol Stream, Illinois 60188. All rights reserved.

Scripture quotations marked TPT are from *The Passion Translation®*. Copyright © 2017, 2018 by Passion & Fire Ministries, Inc. Used by permission. All rights reserved. ThePassionTranslation.com.

Please note that certain pronouns in Scripture that refer to God the Father, Jesus, and the Holy Spirit may differ from some Bible publisher's styles. The name of satan and related names are not capitalized—even to the point of breaking the rules of grammar.

Connect at SparklingBrooks.com | Facebook & Instagram @SparklingBrooks

SPECIAL THANKS

To my Rescuer, Jesus: Thank you for loving me too much to let me stay stuck in the pain of my past. May our journey of healing bring hope to millions—for their healing and freedom, and for your glory.

To my husband, Steve: I know how much God loves me because He gave me you. What a gift! Your kindness, support, and unconditional love are a reflection of His heart. Thank you for giving me space and time to walk the road of healing into the past so that we can have a brighter present and future.

To my boys, Andrew and Christian: Thank you for your encouragement and love. You continually bring a smile to my face and joy to my heart. I am honored to be your mom.

To my parents, James and Sue: Thank you for never giving up on me, for your constant prayers, and for the reciprocal gift of forgiveness.

To my tribe: Thank you for being rope holders and prayer partners, and for grabbing the hand of Jesus too. Thank you for honoring and celebrating the journey alongside me and for loving me just as I am, right where I am—yesterday, today, and tomorrow.

CONTENTS

FOREWARD

My husband and I had several hours of night driving ahead of us. Relaxing in the passenger seat, it was the perfect opportunity to read a portion of *Jesus and Me*. It didn't take long for emotions to come up. Right there in the car I sensed the Presence of Jesus. He helped me find divine perspective concerning a difficult situation in my life journey. He gave a fresh lens to see truth, and the sting of a painful memory was lifted.

The healing love of Jesus is the heartbeat of this book. Kimberly invites us into her sacred story of discovery and encounter in the Secret Place. She models and systematically guides us down a path of transformation from brokenness to restoration. Through Biblically anchored truths, we learn how to creatively connect with our Wonderful Counselor and Prince of Peace.

As a practicing psychotherapist, I'm excited to have this additional tool in my toolbox along with a new, quality resource to recommend for clients.

Get ready...greater levels of freedom await you as you experience the faithful love and healing of Jesus!

Donna Jaree Brooks, MA, LCPC
Psychotherapist
Songwriter/Worship Leader
THREE O'CLOCK SESSION

INTRODUCTION

I know her. She is my daughter. I know the book you hold in your hands was not easy for her to write. In telling her story, she has poured out large portions of her heart and soul, portions that came with a price.

As you read this book, I pray that you will find an amazing truth that will completely change your life. The heart-cry of most of us is to be free from that which holds us captive. The great difficulty is that we often cannot recognize how or when pain bound us. If we do, we do not know how to find the healing and freedom we need to move forward.

I am proud of my daughter's authenticity and courage to share her journey with you. Steeped in love and scripture, she shares how you can gain and enjoy the tremendous freedom that is available to all. Freedom is more than just a word—freedom is a Person. A Person you will meet on the pages of *Jesus and Me*, a Person who can set you free from pain, restore your heart, and release your destiny. May John 8:32 & 36 come to life for you as you walk your personal journey into healing, into truth, and into freedom.

"Then you will know the truth, and the truth will set you free...if the Son sets you free, you will be free indeed."

James LeCrone
Dad and Champion
Pastor, Metropolitan Baptist Church
Decatur, Illinois

~ A PERSONAL NOTE TO YOU ~

In the past, I have sometimes found myself (okay, a lot of times) afraid to be vulnerable and choosing not to use my voice. Jesus brought that to my attention one day. I knew, in His love, He wanted to get to the root of it—me, not so much. After weeks of keeping busy, my go-to when I do not want to do something, I finally surrendered and sank into my favorite chair with my journal in hand.

Jesus began walking me back through various memories. We eventually came to the time when I first became a victim at a young age. That was where I first believed that I was powerless and had no choice but to "stay silent and do nothing." That was the day, in fear and confusion, the little girl in me gave up her voice.

Oh, but Jesus. He is the Redeemer. The Healer. The Restorer.

Not only has He healed and redeemed those painful moments in my life, but also has given me back my voice. No longer do I live out of reaction to painful events and fear; I live knowing that I am who my Heavenly Father says I am.

He has lifted off the bands that gripped my mind of victim mentality and brought me to sit with Him in Heavenly places. I am His, and He is mine. He is my safe place and the One who continually sings a love song over my life.

As I have walked out my healing journey with Jesus, I have come to learn that He never wastes an experience. When I asked Him not to waste any of mine, He smiled. He already had a plan. Together, we have written this book.

We have written it for you.

May it bring hope, help, and encouragement as you walk out your own journey of healing and freedom with the One who can restore your heart and release your destiny.

Much love,

Kimberly Ann Weber

PART I

My Story of Love, Healing, and Freedom

CHAPTER ONE

End of My Rope

S itting on the edge of the bed, I stared blindly at my bedroom wall clenching the phone so hard my hand hurt.

Three rings. Four rings. I waited for her to answer.

I had broken down and finally called her. My mother.

She would know what to do. She would know how to pray. She would know what to say to talk me away from the edge of the deep crevice into which I was about to fall.

She answered. She was home to me. At the sound of her voice, my emotions overflowed, and tears spilled down my cheeks. My world was falling apart once again.

The words stuck in my throat like glue. I finally forced them out, "It happened again!"

"What happened again?" she softly asked.

"A car wreck. Someone hit me from behind. *Again!*"

I could almost feel the air whooshing out of her lungs across the long-distance line, "Are you okay?" Concern vibrated in her voice.

"No."

I struggled to breathe. It had been fifteen years, and I was *still* recovering from the first accident that had turned my world upside down. My world was spiraling out of control, once again. My father-in-law was gravely ill, and a young family member had been diagnosed with a terminal illness; now another car accident. It was the perfect storm.

3

The latest car accident triggered something inside of me. My soul screamed, "I can't go back there again. I can't handle additional trauma to my body, my brain, or my emotions. I may not make it back this time!"

Fear wrapped itself around me like a straightjacket. A picture swirled forward in my mind and tumbled out my mouth. "Mom, help me! I feel like I'm clinging to a long rope that is dangling off the side of a cliff..."

The scene continued to play out in my mind and I saw myself sliding down to the frayed edges of the rope's end. My fingers tightened their hold around the phone as if to keep me from losing my grip and dropping into the dark crevice looming beneath me.

"Mom...I'm afraid. I'm afraid someone above is going to cut the rope instead of pulling me back up to safety. Mom...will you say a prayer for me?"

She did. It calmed me; for a little while.

CHAPTER TWO

He Loves Me?

The peace from Mom's prayer wore off, and days later I again found myself desperately clinging to the frayed edges of the rope.

I was an emotional and physical mess. Not just from the recent accident, but emotional scars and injuries from the first accident were still present, reminding me daily what I had suffered. I had spent years in doctors' offices, seeing neurologists, physical therapists, chiropractors, and doing therapy exercises in hopes that my brain would rewire itself from the damage of the head trauma. After fifteen years, I was still fighting vertigo, memory loss, migraines, pain, and limited range of motion in my neck. I could only rotate my head twenty degrees each way to the right and to the left.

A friend, knowing my fragile state of mind, told me about private prayer appointments at the church we were attending. She made the appointment for me. It was only out of desperation that I agreed to go. I did not know it at the time, but I was about to experience part of the Lord's Prayer—*on Earth as it is in Heaven*—an experience that would beautifully wreck me in a good way.

Raised in a church, I was used to people saying they would pray for me, only to walk away. I never took much stock in the fact that they prayed when they were alone with God. So what would entail a private prayer appointment? Would people silently pray for me or would they pray aloud? Would they say a prayer of blessing and a few kind words and send me on my way? Questions rattled around in my mind. It seemed weird to me, but I was desperate, so I went.

When I arrived, three kind ladies welcomed me and put me at ease. Instantly, I felt safe, safe enough to pour out some of the pain that was strangling my heart and soul. After I shared what I was going through, they explained that they were going to invite Jesus to minister to my heart and my body. I was okay with that. One of the ladies explained she was a massage therapist and asked if she could gently lay her hands on the back of my re-injured neck. I agreed.

It was a Divine setup, one that would challenge old thought patterns and change my paradigm forever.

As she laid her hands on my neck, one of the other ladies smiled and quietly began to pray–aloud. She prayed for peace to abound in the room. It did! A sweet peace settled over me. It seeped into my weary soul, and for the first time in fifteen years, my body began to relax.

As peace permeated the atmosphere, her soft voice once again caught my attention, "I see a picture of you, Kimberly, as a little girl, maybe around four or five years of age. You are wearing a red, white, and blue outfit that looks like an American flag."

Immediately, in my mind, I saw myself as a little girl running in my favorite outfit! The one outfit I begged my mom to let me wear every single day, much to her chagrin. I loved that outfit! It was red, white, and blue and reminded me of an American Flag! How did this stranger know that? How did she know it looked like a flag? How did she know it was my favorite?!

She then began to speak the words of Zephaniah 3:17, "The Lord your God is with you, the Mighty Warrior who saves. He takes great delight in you; in His love, He sings over you and rejoices..." She paused. "Kimberly, God *delights* in you. He *rejoices* over you. He is *singing* over you. God *loves* you!"

The words "God loves you" pierced my heart. It was if an arrow itself carried the words straight into the core of my being. My mind and heart tried to grasp what she was saying, *God Himself...Creator of the Universe...loves me?*

As the revelation of God's love entered my heart, a warmth began to seep into the back of my neck and down my shoulders. Choosing not to fight it, I allowed the peace and love to envelop me. Tears streamed down my face as waves of His love washed over me—over my injured neck, over my body, over my soul, over my heart.

At the end of the prayer time, the massage therapist, who had her hands on my neck, asked if I had noticed the heat and warmth. I nodded not thinking anything of it. I thought she had put some type of warming ointment on my neck—she had not.

Knowingly, she smiled. Unknowingly, I smiled back.

As I walked out of the church that evening and swung open the door, I looked directly to my left and to my right. I gasped. My head moved from side to side! After fifteen years of restricted movement in my neck, I instantly had full-range of motion, and all the pain was gone!

The dam broke. A deluge of hot, salty tears poured down my face, soaking my shirt. For years I had held that flood of tears back trying to keep it all together, trying to be brave, trying not to let others know of my impairment in any way.

I cried all the way home with the words "He loves me?" resonating in my heart. My heart was experiencing something new, and my mind was wrestling with it. Growing up, I believed God to be the Judge on His big throne ready to punish me if I did anything wrong. So who was *this* God who sang over me? Who delighted in me? Was it true? Did He genuinely love me just as I was...hurt, broken, damaged, and full of fear and shame?

Emotionally spent, I walked into the house and climbed into bed. What I had just experienced was real and personal. I did not want the feeling of love, acceptance, and peace to leave nor did I want anyone to take it away from me. Blowing my red nose, I wiped the tears from my swollen eyes, laid my head on my pillow, and closed my eyes.

Immediately, in my mind, I saw an outline of a door appear far away in the distance. The door began to open from my side and light beyond the door spilled into the darkness surrounding me. The silhouette of the person opening the door came into focus.

Jesus had come for me when I was too wrapped up in pain and darkness to open the door myself. Without saying a word, He motioned with His head toward the light. The motion that said, "Come with me."

I whispered, "If this is who you truly are, I will go with you—anywhere."

CHAPTER THREE

Do You Trust Me?

For days, I basked in my new-found wonder. My neck remained healed, and I still felt the love poured into me at the prayer appointment. I began to wonder if the love and healing would go away if I did something wrong. I started to question why I was just now experiencing this immense love and acceptance. I had asked Jesus into my heart when I was five. John 3:16 had been one of the first Bible verses I memorized as a kid.

> *For God so loved the world that he gave his one and only Son, that whoever believes in him shall not perish but have eternal life.*

However, this was different. I was *experiencing* Jesus' love. Jesus was no longer just a person who came to earth more than 2,000 years ago for all humanity; He was personal to me, in the here and now. Jesus was no longer mere head knowledge. I was experiencing Him in my heart.

From the first taste of His healing, His love, and His goodness, I longed for more. I would lie in bed at night and ask Him to show me who He was to me. I began to hear little whispers in my spirit, and Jesus and I started having short conversations. At first, I wondered if I was making it all up, but I was not one to usually have conversations with myself. His voice was always kind, and I felt safe. One day, while I was singing in the shower, He interrupted my song and thoughts.

"Do you trust me?"

Fear slowly crept its way up my body, and I stopped singing. Not because He had spoken to my heart; I was getting used to that. It was because He caught me off guard, directly in an area I did not want to go.

Holding my breath until my lungs hurt, I knew I had a choice to make. I could ignore Jesus, I could lie to Him, or I could be honest — with Him and with myself. I felt the weight of the question hanging in the steamy air. I decided to be honest.

"No. I don't trust you," I blurted.

Tears streamed down my face mixing with the water beating down from the showerhead. I knew I was at a crossroad. Trust. That was no easy thing. I lost trust in people and God at an early age. I had been hurt, manipulated, and disappointed. Questions raced through my mind. *Was Jesus trustworthy? Would I give Him the chance to earn my trust? Was I brave enough to be vulnerable? Was I capable of opening up to the One who was beginning to win my heart?*

At that time, I did not truly understand the full importance of trusting Him, but He did. He knew that where He needed to go, deep in my heart, would require me to trust Him—completely. If I did not trust Him, I would not allow Him to go there. If He did not go there, my heart would not be fully restored.

He desired to redeem and restore places that had been wounded and nearly destroyed, but I had to be willing to let Him go into those places. I had to be willing to let Him take me back to them. It would require me to be brave, something I was not quite ready for and honestly, did not think I was capable of doing.

Time and time again, He whispered, "Do you trust me?"

Time and time again, I answered honestly, "No."

Gaining my trust was a process. I wish I could say it was a short one. It was not. Jesus had layers of mistrust to remove, but over time, as I experienced more of His gentle love, my honest "no" started to turn to an honest "yes," and I began to trust Him with pieces of my past and portions of my heart. I began to trust that He truly loved me for who I was, not for what He wanted or expected me to do. I started to see and believe that He was for me and saw me differently than I or anyone else saw me. I began to trust the Person who was determined to show me who He truly was.

I began to trust that He was good.

CHAPTER FOUR

The Blue Shoes

My early years consisted of memorizing Bible verses in a Bible-based church; a great foundation and heritage for which I am incredibly grateful. Looking back, I realized how much of my church upbringing, unfortunately, was also based on rules and performance. Follow the rules, earn approval. Break the rules, be shamed or punished. Deeply etched in my mind were all the things I was not allowed to do; the reasons, not so much. Part of "being good" included reading the Bible, dressing a certain way, not going to certain places and avoiding certain things, all of which made a person acceptable with a nicely applied label of "good Christian."

The rules, not the Person, became the focus. Without the love, grace, and Spirit, it became a faulty religion, not an actual relationship with Jesus. I do not remember learning about the Holy Spirit or that the gifts mentioned in the Bible are for today, and when I realized there was more, I felt sad that something and Someone so precious had been kept from me.

At the age of ten, I became a preacher's kid, a "PK," living in a glass house. What my brothers and I did and how we acted was considered a reflection of the pastor. It did not take long for this people-pleasing kid to learn to follow the rules. My young heart believed that if I behaved and did good things, I would be accepted by others, not rejected. Loved, not punished. It was all based on my doing. I learned to control people's view of me by my actions.

That belief carried over into my adult years, and years of living out of that belief laid down deep grooves in my track of performance-based thinking.

The deep-ingrained grooves hindered my ability to accept the truth that Jesus loved me and accepted me as I was, even when I did wrong, made wrong choices, and lived in the consequences of my actions.

One day, as I was spending some quiet time with Him, He whispered, "I enjoy giving you gifts." Unintentionally, I shook my head and brushed away what He said with a nonchalant "Okay." He was persistent and determined to get His point across. "Kimberly, it's My nature. It's My delight to surprise you with good things; beautiful things." He stopped. I was silent. After a few moments, He continued with greater emphasis, "I do it because of who I am, not because of what you do."

I did not want to be rude, so I did not say it aloud, but I was thinking, *Yeah, right.*

A few days later, as I pulled into one of my favorite department stores, I heard Him insist He had a surprise for me. As I parked the car, He excitedly whispered, "Go to the shoe aisle." Of course, what woman would not want to hear that? However, I was there to buy a gift for a friend; I did not need another pair of shoes, I did nothing to earn a pair of shoes, and I had not asked for a new pair of shoes.

I ignored Him.

I chose the gift for my friend and made my way to the checkout lane, reasoning that I had probably heard wrong or made it all up in my head. Curiosity, however, got the best of me, and I found myself making a detour and meandering my way into the shoe aisle.

Highlighted—like a spotlight from Heaven—sat a pair of beautiful, high-heeled, blue-suede sandals. One pair. The only pair like them in the store. (I know, I looked.) Size 7. Suede. Blue. My favorite color.

I tried them on. The sandals fit perfectly. For a few moments, I felt like Cinderella, and then I tumbled right back into the groove of performance-based thinking. I did not earn them or deserve them. I returned them to the shelf, reasoning I was selfish. I was there to buy a gift for a friend, not myself.

As I walked away, a feeling of sadness came over me. Somehow I knew it was Jesus' sadness I was feeling along with my own. I did not think I deserved them. I doubted that I deserved Him. I began to wonder if I would ever have enough faith. *Would I ever have enough faith to believe that I was enough? Would I ever have enough faith to trust Him? Would I ever have enough faith to believe that He was good?*

Turning down an aisle, a woman blocked my path with her cart. In no hurry to move, she *slowly* went through the blouses hanging on the rack— one-by-one-by-one. Jesus was giving me more time to think about it. I sighed, turned the cart around, marched back to the shoe aisle, and grabbed the beautiful shoes off the shelf. I was still unsure of what I did to deserve them.

Within five minutes of purchasing them and leaving the store, the war in my mind began...*Kimberly, you just made that entire thing up to justify buying a new pair of shoes. Jesus does not care about things like that. Other people are starving, and you think He wants to give you a pair of shoes? He does not even really talk to you!*

My thoughts continued to beat me up as I drove to another destination across town. Dejectedly, I walked into the next store. Glancing at a display sign my heart lifted and I began to laugh. Aloud. I did not care who heard me or who saw me. An artist had painted a pair of high-heeled shoes on the sign along with the words:

> **Every woman needs a good pair of shoes...**
> **to go with her faith.**

As I laughed, a wave of His love washed over me. Those beautiful blue-suede sandals *were* for me, and they were from Jesus. They were a gift. He gave them because that is who He is; a Giver of good gifts. He has been from the beginning of time. He gave the gift of Himself on the cross.

The revelation of the goodness of His nature unlocked my heart and settled in my mind. It broke through the faulty thought pattern and the lie I believed that I had to *do something to get something.*

Today, I wear His gift proudly. Those blue-suede sandals remind me that Jesus cares for me on a personal level. Those sandals accessorize my faith—faith to believe that He does speak to me, that I do hear Him, that I am enough, and that I am worthy of His good gifts. You, my friend, are worthy of them, too.

We need merely to receive.

CHAPTER FIVE

Come Closer

As my relationship with Jesus deepened, I became more accustomed to hearing His voice in my spirit. I also became more inquisitive about *seeing* Him in my mind the way I had the night I closed my eyes and saw Him open the door and beckon me to follow Him into the light.

I had not used my imagination to visualize in years. As a young child, the enemy hijacked it early with thoughts and images that caused me great fear. My mind, wanting to protect me, put up walls of protection around my imagination, and I used it less and less. Jesus was slowly gaining more of my trust, and one day, I asked Him if He would show me more about Him—just a bit. One evening, He did.

My favorite time to spend with Jesus was right before going to sleep. That night, I had gotten my two sons settled into their beds, climbed into my own, turned on my worship music, opened my Bible and journal, and closed my eyes to pray. To my surprise, I found myself sitting on Jesus' lap. As I sat on His lap, I looked down and noticed I was wearing a white dress and seemed to be around the age of seven. Jesus' arms were tightly around me as I sat sideways, intently studying the bright light on the giant throne next to us. I knew it was God, but I felt so secure sitting in the lap of Jesus that I was not afraid.

We sat there for a while, in perfect peace. Then Jesus said, "I want to introduce you to the Father."

I stiffened, "Ummm, no. I'm happy sitting right here with you."

In my heart, I knew Jesus loved me. He was the one gaining my trust. I was afraid of God! I had no desire to meet the Judge from whom I had spent most of my life hiding. I had feared that my actions would anger or disappoint God, and He would use His big stick to get me back in line. Nope! I was content sitting with Jesus. He was the safe one. I snuggled closer and sat very still.

Jesus also sat quietly, and I could feel His accepting love. He did not seem disappointed that I did not want to meet the Father; nor did He condemn or shame me into it. He continued to hold me with His arms securely around me. After a while, I timidly whispered, "Okay, but only if you go with me."

I sensed His heart swell with joy. Standing, He placed me on the floor next to Him. Taking my hand, we began walking toward the Father. As we approached the throne, I began to pull away. *What was I thinking? Meeting God was a bad idea! Jesus tricked me into feeling safe with Him, and now God was about to punish me!*

I think it was God in His kindness who allowed me to watch the scene unfold from afar. From a distance, I saw God, Jesus, and myself all as figures of light. Father God stood and walked the short distance to Jesus and me. God reached out His hand...and gently touched my lips.

I let out my breath. Father God had gently touched my lips, and I was still alive. I did not die, nor did He show any anger toward me. The wonder of it all was too much. I opened my eyes and focused on my Bible and journal beside me, my mind sorting out what had just happened. The words from Paul in Second Corinthians chapter 12 came to mind where Paul talks about having visions and revelations from the Lord. He goes on to describe a person taken up to the third heaven, "Whether it was in the body or out of the body I do not know - God knows."

Stunned, I pondered if I had just had a vision. I had been with Jesus, in His lap as a young girl, sitting next to God on His throne of light. Jesus had introduced me to His Father, who was also *my* Heavenly Father. The Heavenly Father who loved me unconditionally. The Heavenly Father I was meant to know personally. John 20:17 came to life.

"I am ascending to my Father and your Father,
to my God and your God."

From that moment, my perspective of God began to change. After Jesus introduced me to Him, I found myself less afraid and began to wonder what God was like as the Father. I would occasionally close my eyes and ask Jesus to take me back to Father God and the throne room, which He did. When I was there, I often saw other people, as figures of light, standing before the throne, singing and worshiping. I always made sure to stand in the far back. I was not completely sure of Him. Plus, I was still looking for the big stick; He could have it hidden out of sight.

I never wanted to go closer than the back row, but sometimes wondered if He would see me or remember that Jesus had introduced me to Him.

> *And he said, Hear thou therefore the word of the LORD: I*
> *saw the LORD sitting on his throne, and all the host of heaven*
> *standing by him on his right hand and on his left*
> *(1 Kings 22:19 KJV).*

One particular time, as I envisioned standing behind thousands of other people before the throne of God, I had an overwhelming urge to jump up and down to the beat of a lively song. As the music around the throne swelled, the urge within me grew stronger. I gave in and jumped—just a little. It was more like a hop. That one hop led to others and gave me a boldness to jump a little higher. Before I knew it, my arm shot straight up in the air, like a little kid desperate to get picked for the last game of Red Rover. Jumping higher, I yelled above the crowd, "Pick me! Pick me! Pick me!"

A verse floated across my memory.

> *"See, this has touched your lips; your guilt is taken away and*
> *your sin atoned for." Then I heard the voice of the Lord saying,*
> *"Whom shall I send? And who will go for us?" And I said,*
> *"Here am I. Send me!" (Isaiah 6:7-8)*

I recalled the time Jesus took me to meet Father God, and God touching my lips. The realization that God had already chosen me settled in my heart, but how could I be sent when I was broken? An urgency to be clean rose within me, and the weight and consequences of being damaged by others along with my own bad choices threatened to pull me into a pit of despair. *Would Jesus be able to clear out all the junk that had piled up in my heart and soul? Would He be able to clean me, heal me, and restore me? Would He want to do so? Was His love great enough? Was I worth that much to Him? Would He be able to dismantle the fortress holding me captive? Was it safe to let down the thick walls of self-protection? Could I trust Him with the rooms of resentment, hurt, rejection, abandonment, and trauma?*

Fear and trauma were the foundation of my fortress, and I knew the dismantling and rebuilding would unbury deep layers of both. I desperately wanted to believe that Jesus could heal me and bring me into the fullness that He promised in His Word: a life abundant in Him. Since first experiencing His love and the miraculous healing of my neck, I had told Jesus I would go with Him anywhere. I determined to hold true to my word and trust Him once again, even if it meant going deep within my soul, deep into the painful memories of my past.

CHAPTER SIX

The Perfect Father

I t had been a busy week, and I was looking forward to spending some uninterrupted quiet time with Jesus. I had barely snuggled under the covers when I heard Him whisper in my heart.

"Do you trust Me?"

I paused, wondering where this was going. My trust in Jesus and His goodness was deepening, and I whispered a hesitant, "Yes."

"You need to forgive your father."

"What?!"

"It is time to forgive your father."

"I can't do that," I softly whispered aloud. "And why are you messing up our sweet, quiet time with this?! You didn't even say hello!"

Thankfully, by then, I had come to accept His pure and loving intentions. He always spoke to me in a quiet voice and had patience with me. Slowly, I was beginning to understand that Jesus knew when and what I needed to do to move forward in my healing journey. He always desired healing and freedom for me, His beloved.

He waited.

I let out a deep sigh as an inward struggle ensued. Too much time had gone under the bridge. However, Jesus' words caused the reserve of hurt and anger that had been buried deep within to start to rise to the surface. As it forced its way to the top, the four-year-old in me cried out, "Why didn't he know what was going on? Why didn't he protect me?"

The bitter teenager in me cried, "Why did he always put the ministry before me? Why did I have to be good to earn his love and acceptance? Why couldn't I have it regardless of what I did or didn't do?"

The young adult in me cried out, "Why did he turn his back on me when I didn't live up to his expected standards? Yes, I chose to live with someone outside of marriage, but dads aren't supposed to turn their backs on their daughters."

Once my tirade began, I could not stop the volcanic explosion; the lid was off, and it all came pouring out. I found myself drowning, the covers soaked in pain and tears. As the weeping subsided, a glimmer of truth turned on inside my heart. My entire life, I had held my parents to unattainable standards. I had expected *them* to be perfect. I never thought about the environments in which they had been raised and trained. This new realization did not make everything all right; it just helped me understand and make room for grace. It was in the fabric of the past; the past that Jesus was bringing to the present so that He could move me into my future.

"I still can't do it," I whispered. "I don't have the strength to forgive him."

"What if I go with you? Like the time I introduced you to the Father."

Looking back, I realized Jesus did not say, "Let's do this in the throne room." That would have intimidated me. His statement simply directed me there. Emotionally exhausted, I agreed and closed my eyes. I found myself standing next to dad, a few feet away on my right. Jesus was standing next to me on my left. The three of us were directly in front of God, who again was light, sitting on a throne of light.

With Jesus by my side prompting me, I turned and told my dad I forgave him. I forgave him for his absence when I needed him. I forgave him for leaving me unprotected. I forgave him for turning his back on me and rejecting me. I forgave him for not being perfect.

Jesus took my hand and looked at the perfect Father. I looked up at Him, too. I began to weep again. No one had taught me to do what I was about to do. I just knew I needed to do it to be genuinely free. Between sobs, I blurted out, "Father God, please don't hold anything against dad on my account; of things he didn't do right that impacted me and my life."

Bitter, scalding tears I had held in for years continued to flow until none were left. It was finished. I had let the anger, bitterness, and resentment go. I had let dad go. I had allowed him out of the prison I had kept him locked in deep within my heart.

The rooms of resentment, rejection, and bitterness toward my father all emptied through the door of forgiveness.

Jesus' love had taken me to that place. He began to fill those now-empty rooms with His love, acceptance, and peace. His love had won! Not just His love, but the perfect Father's love.

Later, as I reflected on my time in the throne room forgiving my dad, Jesus brought back the memory of my dad coming to my apartment asking for forgiveness for turning his back on me. I was in my early twenties, and my heart was too broken and hurt to forgive or move toward restoration. Years had gone by since that day. In Jesus' perfect time, within hours, He cleaned out and restored years of damage caused by hurt, wrongdoings, and misunderstandings.

As Jesus and I continued to have conversations about my dad and me, I began to realize that God was the only perfect Father. I started to see my earthly father from a different perspective. He loved God. He loved his family. He loved me. Were his actions right all of the time? No; neither were mine. I forgave myself for my wrongs and asked my dad to forgive me, too.

Although I did not realize it at the time, Jesus knew I saw the Heavenly Father based on my experience in life with my earthly father. I was projecting my reality on earth onto the Persons of the Trinity—God the Father, God the Son (Jesus), and God the Spirit (the Holy Spirit).[1] My earthly father represented the father figure of God to me. Jesus, in His love, walked me through the truth of who my Heavenly Father is and through the beautiful process of restoration.

With all the resentment and hurt gone, I was able to love my dad with the love Jesus put in my heart. God's love was changing both our hearts on parallel paths. Today, my dad and I are on similar journeys filled with *experiencing* who God the Father is and His amazing love. When I need him, dad is present. He listens, comforts, and blesses me and the story God is continuing to unfold in my life.

Soon after that experience, I realized I no longer feared God anymore, and it just seemed natural for me to call Him "Papa." Some may think that calling God "Papa" is sacrilegious. I think it is beautiful and that He enjoys His children calling Him "Papa," "Abba," or "Daddy." He is the perfect Father and wants a close relationship with His children. That is why Jesus, God's only Son, came to earth and took our place on the cross. He was perfect, yet He suffered all the punishment we deserved. He did it for me, and He did it for you. He did it in love so we could accept His gift and walk into the throne room and sit on Papa's lap. I am thankful that Jesus' love won on the cross and is still winning today.

Looking back over the years, I now see ways the enemy whispered lies about my identity, about my worth, and about my parents' love for me. He used multiple tactics to dig a chasm between them and me. He would whisper lies such as, "They don't really care about you or what is happening in your life. They don't understand you. They don't even love you unless you are good." Satan is a destroyer of hearts, lives, and relationships (John 10:10). He does not want a family intact. He knows a family unit has strength and is a picture of God's complete love. God is love, and Abba longs for His family to be whole. He loves you and me. His heart is for each of us to be part of His family.

A father and mother are important. My heart breaks for everyone, young and old, who has experienced neglect and rejection; those who have felt abandoned and unsafe; those who have suffered physical, emotional, and verbal abuse; and those who have had words of hate instead of words of life and validation spoken to them. Please know that is *not* the heart of the Heavenly Father. That is not who He is. That is not how He intended you to be treated.

God designed you in love, to be loved.

I pray that even as you read this now, you hear His gentle voice telling you that you, too, are worth every drop of blood that spilled from Jesus' body on the cross when He came to restore your relationship with the perfect Father. You are and will continue to be the joy set before Jesus that gave Him the strength to stay on the cross until it was finished.

Jesus is the only way to the perfect Father.

His love won on the cross, for you.

His love for you is not in vain.

His love says, "You are worth it."

CHAPTER SEVEN

The Bathtub

Growing up, I had a sense that I always had to take care of myself. If someone offered to help me when I needed it, fine, but I never asked anyone for help. I was determined to make it on my own. As an adult, I usually had a full-time and a part-time job and made sure I had enough money in the bank in case I lost one of those jobs. I was self-sustaining and kept a separate bank account even after my husband and I married. I wanted to make sure I could make it on my own regardless of my circumstances.

One day, Jesus wanted to talk to me about my independent nature. At the time, I saw nothing wrong with my independence reasoning that He had made me that way, so when He asked me if I wanted to know why I was independent, I quickly said, "Sure!"

Unbeknownst to me, He had plans to open the door to the room of abandonment. He did it by taking me back to a childhood memory; one that had been buried in my subconscious since I was five. I had not thought about that traumatic day in years.

I was five-years-old playing in the bathtub at our red brick home in the country. The water in the bathtub had grown cold, and not being allowed to turn on the hot water, I called for mom to add some more.

"Mom!"

No answer.

I called out for dad.

No answer.

The house was strangely silent. More time passed. I continued to call out, with no answer from either of them. I knew they were home. Thoughts of what I had heard at church started swirling in my young, vulnerable mind. The rapture had taken place! My young imagination spun out of control as I listened to the lies whispered by the father of lies. *I wasn't good enough! I had been left behind. By my parents. By Jesus!*

I panicked.

Shivering in the bathtub, I screamed for my parents for what seemed like hours. *Had I been bad? Is that why Jesus left me behind? How was I, a little girl, going to survive in the big, scary world all by myself?*

That incident happened forty years prior, and I could not remember how I got out of the tub. Jesus, however, had a plan to show me that He was with me and reframe that traumatic memory into a place of peace. When Jesus asked me to think back on the memory again, I found my five-year-old self sitting in the cold water of the bathtub shivering, my voice hoarse from screaming, and feeling alone and scared. Someone walked through the bathroom door.

It was Jesus. He sat on the floor next to the bathtub.

"You're safe," He consoled me in a soft voice. "You're not alone. I'll stay with you until your parents return." A sense of peace settled over me. Jesus was present. Others were not, but He was.

"You didn't leave me?" I sobbed.

"No, I didn't leave you. You belong to me. I would never leave you behind."

"Will...will...will you do some of your magic and fill the tub with warm water?" I stammered as I tried to dry my eyes with wet hands.

Jesus laughed, "Well, in Heaven, we don't call it magic. We call it a miracle."

I did not see Jesus turn on the hot water, but the tub was instantly full of warm water and lots of bubbles. He sat and talked to me until the door of the bathroom opened and my dad walked in. My dad had come for me! He lifted me out of the tub and wrapped me in a big, white towel.

Whenever I look back on the event now, I see Jesus sitting with me, performing one of His miracles. By taking me back to that memory and showing me He was present, He reframed that memory into a lasting promise, one now built with walls of faith and trust, knowing He will never leave me.

Once the truth that Jesus and my parents had not abandoned me displaced the lie I had believed since I was five, I found myself no longer reacting and making decisions based on my subconscious belief that I had to take care of myself. Jesus showed me that even if others left, He would always be with me; He would never leave me behind. Knowing that in my heart gave me the courage to start trusting others to be there for me as well.

I am so thankful for God's good gifts, despite my actions or where I am in life. He gave me the most caring, patient, unselfish, and giving person I have ever known as a husband. Steve has lived with me during my entire healing journey. I know he is part of God's plan and a special gift to me. Jesus in His perfect timing uncovered the faulty belief that I had to take care of myself. That was fifteen years into our marriage. The week after Jesus healed and reframed that memory I went to the bank and added Steve to the bank account I had been keeping only in my name, just in case he left me.

That was a big moment for me; a declaration that I was giving up my self-sufficiency and trusting Steve to stay with me, to be faithful to his word. I was choosing to trust him, no strings attached.

Jesus' love won—again. It continues to prevail as He continues to show me I can trust Him and the people He has put in my life. Even if people around me go about their business and I feel ignored or forgotten, He is with me—always present, always near. I do not have to scream for His help. He hears the slightest whispers of my heart. The room filled with the fear of being abandoned and left behind is now filled with Jesus, family, and friends.

"Never will I leave you; never will I forsake you"
(Hebrews 13:5).

For those wondering, I later asked my mom about the bathtub incident. Her sisters had come to town, and she had gone shopping with them, leaving me in the bathtub thinking dad would get me out. He was outside working, and she had forgotten to tell him.

I forgave her, too.

CHAPTER EIGHT

The Wedding Dress

With each layer of healing, I fell more in love with Jesus. I learned that I could not only trust Him, but also His timing and His process. Over time, He was clearing out, reframing, and remodeling the rooms of my heart. If He had done it all at once, or even one room right after the other, I do not think that I would have fully recovered. After each room, He let me soak in my new found healing and freedom. He gave me time to adjust and accept the truth that He was planting both in my heart and in my mind.

During one of my quiet times, I closed my eyes and found myself in a garden. Someone was putting flowers in my hair, and I realized I was wearing a white wedding dress. Excitement built up inside of me as I began walking down the aisle toward the person waiting. My heart dropped. *Jesus* was standing up front waiting to take my hand.

Panic rose up within me as I reasoned why I could not take His hand. I was unclean and unworthy. Jesus deserved a spotless bride, and that had been taken away from me when I was young. The poor choices I had made as a young adult added to the parade of shame as I tried to earn acceptance in the arms of others. Ashamed, I turned and ran back up the aisle.

It was days before I could talk to Him again. He may have been ready to work on that room in my heart, but I was not. I was afraid. I did not want to face the shame. I did not want to go back, but deep inside I knew that until I let Him go there, I would not be free of the painful memories that held me captive. I was stuck—a prisoner of my past.

I wanted to be free, but what if Jesus was upset that I had let it happen? That I had not stopped it? What would my parents think? What would my husband think? What would my friends think? It was a secret I had kept locked inside of me since I was a little girl. I know, if it were me reading someone else's story right now, I would be screaming out loud.

"You were a child. You were four!"

Yes, but after years of believing the whispers and threats of shame from the enemy, the secret became part of my DNA, DNA that screamed: "Do Not Access." I was not letting Jesus into this room. It held too much pain, and I felt ashamed and dirty when I thought about it. I questioned whether He would redeem me from this one. His love, however, was determined to win, and a few weeks later, He caught me off guard. My reserves were down, and He walked right in.

I was at an event on finding rest, which seems pretty safe, right? One of the exercises was to put one's self in the Bible story as the facilitator read it aloud. It was the story of Bartimaeus, the blind man who was sitting along the roadside begging when Jesus and His disciples passed. I could choose to be Bartimaeus, one of His disciples, or someone in the crowd. Not comfortable standing out, I decided to be someone in the crowd.

When the speaker began to read the story, I found myself, as a little girl, standing along the side of the road, wearing a stained, dirty dress.

Then they came to the city of Jericho. When He was leaving the town with His followers and many people, a blind man was sitting by the road. He was asking people for food or money as they passed by. His name was Bartimaeus, the son of Timaeus. He heard that Jesus of Nazareth was passing by. He began to speak with a loud voice, saying, "Jesus, Son of David, take pity on me!" Many people spoke sharp words to the blind man telling him not to call out like that. But he spoke all the more. He said, "Son of David, take pity on me." Jesus stopped and told them to call the blind man. They called to him and said, "Take hope! Stand up, He is calling for you!" As he jumped up, he threw off his coat and came to Jesus. Jesus said to him, "What do you want me to do for you?" (Mark 10:46-52)

As Jesus and His disciples walked by me, I somehow got the courage like Bartimaeus and quietly cried out His name. Hearing my slight whimper, He stopped and searched the crowd. His eyes settled on me, standing on the edge. He walked over to me and knelt down, face to face. Reaching out, He gently took my tear-stained, dirty face in His clean hands and kindly asked, "What is it you want me to do for you, child?"

I let out a sob, "Make me whole again."

Without saying a word, Jesus stood and picked up the dirty little girl and opening the top of His robe, put me, dirty dress and all against His chest. I felt His skin. Then, I dissolved into Him. I became one with Him. I was a part of Him. I was *in* Him. Fear and shame left me. All I felt was love and the warmth and peace of Him changing me from the inside out.

After a few moments, He asked me to put out my arm. He took my hand and pulled me from His chest. I was not a child anymore; I was a young woman standing in front of Him—face to face. In place of the dirty dress, a long, white, flowing dress with gold buttons on top of the shoulders now adorned my body. I was clean! I felt pure and beautiful.

Jesus smiled at me and asked his disciple John to bring me a robe. Returning within moments with a piece of purple material, John fastened it to the gold buttons of my white dress. "Purple, for royalty," he whispered in my ear.

The feeling of the warmth and love of Jesus stayed with me for days as He continued to heal my heart, my mind, and my body. Some may say that He chose to heal me in an unusual way. I do not care. It worked! His ways are not our ways. He knew to what I would respond. He knew what I needed. He knew what would heal me. John 17:21 holds a special place in my heart.

> *"That all of them may be one, Father, just as you are in me and I am in you. May they also be in us so that the world may believe that you have sent me."*

His love knew. His love won. Jesus redeemed me. I was no longer the little girl who carried the shame of being molested and abused. He made me–His beloved–pure and beautiful. He gave me back my dignity.

Jesus can do the same for you.

CHAPTER NINE

Mistaken Identity

Jesus was slowly teaching me about identity. No longer was I the shameful little girl rejected, forgotten, or abandoned. No longer was I the one who had to earn love. I was His beloved—thoroughly loved, fully accepted. Jesus *liked* to spend time with me! I knew that He saw me through His eyes of love. He was not offended by my past or the fact that I did not get things right all the time. We were now in this together—Jesus and me. He knew who I was and who I would be. He knew what was yet to come.

I had let Him into and He had cleaned so many rooms that had been built by self-protection. There was one door, however, painted a different color than the rest, one through which we had not yet ventured. I knew it had something to do with my past but was not sure what. I kept waiting for Jesus to open it and show me what occupied that space. He did not seem in a hurry to do so. Curiosity finally got the better of me, and one day I gathered up my courage and asked Him to show me what was behind the door. Tilting His head, He looked at me. Then shrugged, took my hand, and opened the door. It was not a room, but a long hallway.

We walked down the hall and stepped outside into a parking lot. I was wearing the flowing white dress with the gold buttons that He had given me earlier. Standing side-by-side, I was somewhat confused as to what He wanted to show me. Then I recognized it—the bar. It was the first bar into which I had stepped foot. After a few moments of silence, He softly spoke, "This is where you gave up your identity."

It all came into clear focus. Jesus was right! At the time, I was underage. I was sweating through my coat. *What if the bouncer realized that the driver's license I gave him was not mine? He knew the girl I was with, the one who had supplied the fake driver's license. Surely, I would be okay.* The bouncer let us in, and before I knew it, I was having the time of my life. The preacher's kid had broken free of the rules and regulations. I had my first taste of alcohol. I danced! To rock music!

Little did I know, I was about to trade one set of chains for a heavier set. That night led to a course of events that led me down a dark road. One I was not designed to travel down. The impressionable young lady gave away more of herself to the first guy who showed her attention, and I found myself in a relationship in which I was manipulated, lied to, and threatened. By the time I came to my senses months later, I had little self-worth, hope, or personal value left. I had left a protected world controlled by fear to fearing for my life. I had been running to stay safe and under the radar ever since.

The weight of what I had done settled across my shoulders like a fifty-pound blanket. I had given up my identity by using someone else's. From that decision, I made choices that seemed fun in the moment but hurt me for years. Jesus put His arm around me and pulled me close. "This is not who you are anymore."

"I'm sorry!" I whispered. "I'm sorry I didn't value the person you created me to be!"

"I know. I've forgiven you, but what do you think about forgiving yourself?"

It was a simple question. The fifty-pound blanket draped around my shoulders became even heavier. Jesus explained that it had been put there by the spirit of condemnation. I did not want it around me anymore. I held Jesus' hand and turned to Him. "Will you take it off of me? It is hiding the beautiful dress you gave me!"

Smiling, He lifted off the heaviness of condemnation as I forgave myself. I forgave myself for not trusting my parents and their protective boundaries, for not valuing myself, and for all the wrong choices I had willingly made. That day I realized there is not only power in forgiving others; there is great freedom in forgiving one's self.

As we turned to leave, Jesus put His hand in His pocket and pulled out a driver's license. He handed it to me. I looked at it and laughed with joy. It was mine, and the picture was of me, in my white dress. I felt light and realized His love had won again, this time over the weight of self-condemnation.

I hugged Him, "Thank you."

Hugging me back, He kissed the top of my head, "You're welcome."

I looked up at Him, and He grinned. I had a sense He was about to show me more about my true identity.

CHAPTER TEN

Release of Dreams

Throughout the years, I have come to appreciate the ways the Trinity reaches out to connect with humanity. God's ultimate goal is to be in a relationship with us. It is not that He is lonely or bored, but that He has an immeasurable amount of love and without someone to love, what is the point?

I make room for Jesus not as a chore or duty or to earn approval, but because He has won my heart, and I have fallen in love with Him. Time with Him is special to me. It is personal. Sometimes He leads me in a time of healing; other times He gives me a new perspective about Himself, Father God, the Holy Spirit, others, or myself. Other times, we just sit and enjoy each other's presence.

I still have much to learn and understand about Jesus. Sometimes I feel like I have only grasped one piece of sand on the enormous beach that surrounds the ocean of His love. I am incredibly thankful for the ways in which He reached out and loved me first. Whether it is seeing Him with the eyes of my heart, seeing Him in my memories, through the Bible, or any other way He wants to engage with me, I am open to receiving more of what He has to share.

One summer, I went with a friend on a road trip to a conference. While there, she picked up a book titled *Exploring the Nature and Gifts of Dreams* by James W. Goll. I asked if I could read it on our five-hour car ride home. I consumed it in an hour. Wow, God spoke this way, too? Closing the book, I asked Him to share things with me through dreams. He answered that night.

Keep Your Eyes on Me

In the dream, I walked into a large, brightly-lit classroom full of students sitting at round tables. The tables were piled high with papers. In the front of the room, two people were playing a lively, upbeat duet on a piano. Not sure of what to do, I sat in an empty chair at one of the tables.

Taking notice of me, one of the persons playing the piano stood up, letting the other carry on the tune. It seemed as if they were waiting for me to arrive. The man picked up a large pair of cymbals, brought them over, and handed them to me. Taking them from him, I struggled to hold onto them as they were big and extremely heavy.

He smiled and returned to the front of the class where he picked up a smaller pair of cymbals. Turning to a choir assembled on risers beside the piano, he began directing them with a cymbal in each hand. At certain times during the song, the director clanged his cymbals. When he did, he looked over and nodded for me to do the same. I brought mine together although I was always a few seconds behind him, and *never* on the beat.

At the end of the song, the choir director put his cymbals down. Dismissing the class, he walked toward me. I knew he was disappointed in me as I was never in rhythm with him. I placed my cymbals on the table and started gathering up papers in a semblance of busyness. Stopping me, He turned my face until our eyes met. Before I could apologize, a huge grin broke out across his face.

"It's not about being perfect. You did *exactly* what I wanted you to do. You kept your eyes on Me."

The director glanced down at the large heavy cymbals lying on the table and reiterated, "Always, keep your eyes on Me." My heart leaped inside of me as I realized I was talking to Jesus! He knew I needed that wisdom as part of my foundation. I was about to embark on a new adventure with Him; one that sometimes carried great weight because of what He showed me through dreams. Sometimes He revealed events that were going to happen or concerns needing prayer in regards to individuals and His church.

Through the years, some dreams have been direct and to the point, but the majority of the dreams have been full of symbolism needing interpretation. I love that Jesus was the One who handed me "cymbals" as my first "symbol!" I also love His timing because He then brought someone into my life who was experienced in dreams and dream interpretation. She has become one of my dearest friends, and I am grateful for her mentoring and helping me to see my dreams through God's eyes.

Through the continued seasons of Jesus maturing me in dream interpretation, Jesus and I spent hours together searching out meanings and building our own personal library, which later proved valuable as He developed me in the gift of prophecy: listening to His heart for others and sharing it with them.[2] Jesus shared with me that His heart's desire is to draw us closer to Him by revealing His nature, His character, His goodness, and His love. The more we understand who He is, the more we understand who we are in Him.

Dreams have been an avenue Jesus used to help me see and understand specific areas of struggle in my life. He has shown me how to pray for people and situations. At times, I have conducted warfare in my dreams and watched it play out a few days or weeks later in the natural. Other times, He gives me dreams full of Him and Heaven. Like this one.

Taste & See

> Oh, taste and see that the Lord is good; Blessed is the man who trusts in Him! (Psalm 34:8; NKJV)

For weeks, this verse captivated me. It intrigued me. I saw Jesus with the eyes of my heart,[3] but how did one taste that the Lord was good? I know now that in Hebrew "taste and see" can be translated "perceive and behold," but I did not have a lexicon or concordance back then, so Jesus humored me and gave me more than what I could imagine.

In the dream, I found myself in a beautiful park setting with picnic tables spread atop vividly green, thick grass. Men and women were dressed "to the nines," mingling and listening to heavenly music. As they mingled, they quietly talked to each other and sipped what looked to be champagne from crystal goblets. Peace saturated the air.

Not knowing anyone, I sat at one of the picnic tables wondering if I, too, would be offered a glass of champagne. A person behind me reached over my shoulder and set a large intricately engraved silver goblet in front of me. Gold thick liquid overflowed its brim and splashed onto the table.

"I don't like beer," I muttered.

"Taste and see." The voice behind me held a hint of amusement.

I took a small sip.

It was heavenly! It was sweet, and as I sipped it, the effervescence of the golden liquid rose up and tickled my nose. I never had, nor have I now, tasted anything so deliciously delightful. After a few sips, Jesus sat down next to me, "Are you enjoying a taste of My goodness?"

I laughed.

"Yes!" I exclaimed as my fingers traced the etchings on the outside of the silver goblet.

"I made that for you," He stated matter-of-factly.

Speechless, a sense of wonder came over me, and I woke up.

Oh, how I tried to go back to sleep and re-enter that dream, but to no avail. I had so many questions to ask Jesus! *What was the liquid in the cup? What did the goblet symbolize? What meaning did it have in a Heavenly sense and what did it mean in the natural realm?*

Jesus could have let me stay there, in the dream, and answered all my questions, but He did not, and so my hunt for answers began.

> *It is the glory of God to conceal a matter; to search out a matter is the glory of kings (Proverbs 25:2).*

We had a lot of fun talking about that dream. In my quiet time, I would bring Jesus a meaning of the goblet and liquid. He would laugh and say, "Close, but try again." He finally started telling me if I was "cold, warm, or hot." I finally hit hot. I represented the goblet!

He confirmed, "I've been molding you, purifying you, personally designing you to carry My glory, My Presence: the gold liquid."

> *For we are God's handiwork, created in Christ Jesus to do good works, which God prepared in advance for us to do (Ephesians 2:10).*

He continued, "The engravings in the silver goblet represent the paths you've taken from birth, now, and into the future." I frowned. We both knew

I had walked far away from Him during my early adult years, during my time of "sowing my wild oats."

Knowing my thoughts, He assured me, "I wasn't far away. Plus, all your paths led back to Me."

His words resonated in my heart. He had always been present, watching over me. I wondered from how much He had protected me that I was not aware. I did not want to know. What I did know was that He loved me and that He had the capability to redeem every painful event in my life.

CHAPTER ELEVEN

The Sudden Rescue

Not all my dreams were of Heaven. Some were fraught with fear. From an early age, I had struggled with fear. Fear was even involved in my decision to ask Jesus into my heart at the age of five. The church that my parents attended preached a lot about hell and its horror. The focus was mainly on avoiding hell. The way to do that and get to Heaven was to accept Jesus. That seemed an easy choice for a five-year-old, and I was considering it, until one Sunday evening service. That evening, the church played a movie that showed people being tortured and killed for being Christians. Little children, like me, had their eardrums punctured so they could no longer hear God's word. I am sure my parents did not know what the movie contained, or they would not have let me see it. My dad took me out, but my sensitive eyes had already seen some of those images, and they were burned deep into my memory, and my soul.

For nights, I would lie in bed and wrestle with asking Jesus to come into my heart. My Sunday school teacher had told me Jesus loved me and that He died for me. I did not want to go to hell, but I did not want the alternative either. I agonized for weeks until one night my heart won over my fear, and I cried out, "Jesus, I just want you." I knew that I was His. Little did I know what was going on in the spirit realm; He showed me years later, in a dream.

I was five, and the room in which I was held captive was small, dark, and dismal. The walls were empty with no windows to let in light. Sitting on the end of a single bed, I stared at a television screen full of static mesmerized, frozen in time, unable to move.

Suddenly, the door to the room burst open.

Bam!

The noise from the door forcibly slamming against the wall behind it shook my gaze away from the static. Light flooded the room, illuminating four walls made of charred railroad ties covered in creosote. The smell of the creosote was overpowering.

The light spilling in from the open door beckoned me. I stood up and began walking toward it. As I did so, the walls came to life, screaming and screeching, and swelling with anger. They did not want to let their little captive go.

Fear gripped me, but somehow I kept moving forward toward the light. Determined to keep me in their grasp the walls with one final scream imploded, spilling fire into the room.

Trapped, fear engulfed me as the fire crept closer. Feeling the heat, I closed my eyes as the sounds of the crackling fire made its way toward me.

A slight whimper escaped my lips, "Help me!"

From the open doorway, someone reached through the fire and pulled me out. I was safe in the arms of the Rescuer. Jesus had kicked open the door to the room that once held me captive. He saved me from the fire and the walls threatening to destroy me. He carried me out of the darkness, into the light.

As I wrote the dream in my journal the next morning, Jesus shared with me that the battle for my life started at an early age. Satan had done his best to keep me locked away; he had tried to railroad my life keeping me from Jesus and my destiny. Jesus, determined to rescue His beloved child, did so when I was five. It was the moment I said that I just wanted Him…regardless of the cost.

That dream with the fiery walls had been so intense, so real, that it stayed with me for weeks. Jesus had rescued me, but at the time, fear still tightly gripped me. By this time in my journey, I understood that when Jesus knew I was ready for more healing, He would let that which needed healing surface through another event, a dream, or one of our talks. A few weeks after experiencing the dream He asked *the* question, "Do you trust Me?"

Deep inside I knew He was talking about trusting Him with the fear that had controlled and manipulated me since I was little. It took several days for me to answer Him. Not knowing what I would find, I was not sure I had the courage yet to face it. I was fearful of Fear.

It became a matter of trust. I could stay stuck in the fear or I could trust Him to move me forward – past it.

I finally decided to trust Him, one more time.

CHAPTER TWELVE

The Root of Fear

The memory to which Jesus took me was one I had shared with several close friends, but this time, I was not telling someone the story—I was reliving it. My mom and dad were young in their faith. We had moved to the country, and they were attending a small church near our home. Again, I was a little girl, around four years of age. See the trend here? One Sunday, as we walked into the foyer of the church, my eyes were drawn to a spinner rack holding pamphlets and tracts.

At eye level was a small tract with a picture of a little girl, who looked just like me, sleeping in her bed. Wrapped around the little girl was a giant black and yellow snake, three times the size of the girl. I froze. Our new home in the country had ditches full of snake holes, and the snakes would find their way to our house. An inner voice whispered that snakes would get me, too. They would enter our home and wrap themselves around me at night.

That day, fear slithered its way right into my young mind; and of all places, in a church.

The entire time we lived in the country, going to bed at night terrified me. Before getting into bed, I looked in the closet, under my bed, and under my covers. When I was in bed, I was afraid to move in case the movement would catch the attention of the snakes. The enemy immobilized me with fear. After seeing that tract, I never felt safe. I never felt safe in the one place I should have felt safe as a child, my own home. Satan had stolen my peace of mind and planted a deep root of fear.

Forgiveness was essential along my journey of healing. I needed to forgive to be fully released from the experience and for Jesus to reframe it and fill it with what He wanted to put in its place. I forgave my parents for taking me to that church and allowing me to see the tract. I also forgave the church and those who were responsible for putting the material in front of my sensitive eyes, as well as the people who created the tract.

After I forgave people, I saw my young-self sitting on my twin bed in the country. Jesus came into the room carrying special tools. I watched as He circled the country home sealing up the windows, baseboards, and doors with a special sealant to keep the snakes out. Completing His task, He smiled and climbed into bed next to me. No longer afraid, the four-year-old me snuggled in close, yawned, and drifted off to sleep in peace.

I do not remember my parents talking to me about my fears when I was young. Today, I encourage parents to ask questions when their kids seem fearful; to not discount what they are feeling, what they are seeing, or what they are saying. To a young child, those fears are real, and negative experiences can be traumatic.[4] I also encourage parents whose child is afraid, to walk the child through the exercise of using his imagination to connect with Jesus by inviting the child to close his eyes and picture Jesus in the room. It is beautiful to hear a child explain what Jesus looks like, what He is wearing, and what Jesus is saying. When a child can visualize Jesus protecting him or taking care of the thing that scares him, he realizes that Jesus is bigger than anything fearful that comes his way.

> *"Let the little children come to me, and do not hinder them,*
> *for the kingdom of heaven belongs to such as these"*
> *(Matthew 19:14).*

Young children spend two-thirds of their time using their imaginations.[5] Satan is sneaky. He knows the stages of human development and takes full advantage of young impressionable minds by planting seeds of fear. Children must learn early to combat negative imagery by visualizing Jesus and allowing Jesus to become their safe place, their Protector, the One who seals up the places in their minds where the enemy is trying to enter. Jesus can bring peace as He holds His child close in His arms.

CHAPTER THIRTEEN

Snake-Stomping Boots

Although I had identified the root of fear, deep down I knew Jesus wanted to show me more. I remembered the older boys down the road, catching snakes in the ditch by our home and swinging them above their heads threatening to throw them at me. Several of them did. Snakes would sun themselves on the cement slab that ran between our home and the garage, and they would slither around the foundation of our home hiding in the bushes. I was terrified of the snakes and did not want to play outside.

One day during my quiet time with Jesus, I found myself back at the brick home in the country. I was five and dressed in my favorite outfit that looked like an American flag; the outfit the lady had described the night Jesus healed my neck—the outfit that screamed freedom.

Looking out the living room window, I saw Jesus walking up the driveway. I ran out to meet Him. He laughed and scooped me up and put me on His shoulders. As I sat on His shoulders, He took off my tennis shoes and slipped on a pair of tall, dark blue rubber boots with white flowers painted on them.

"Oh wow, thanks, Jesus! What are they for?"

He explained as He walked toward the road, me sitting high on his shoulders. "These boots are a present from Me. I made them myself, just for you." He was always giving me the best presents! I am thankful He showed me early on in our relationship that He loved being a Gift Giver. I had become an excellent "gift receiver."

Jesus held my feet in front of Him and admired the boots. He seemed proud of His handiwork. I sat on His shoulders with my legs sticking out admiring them too. When we got to the road, He continued, "These are snake-stomping boots. You don't have to be afraid to play outside anymore. You can stomp on their heads. Nothing can bite you through these."

"Does this mean you're going to put me down now?" I asked apprehensively. We had reached the ditch with snake holes, and I did not want to get down off His shoulders.

He squeezed my ankles, "Only when you are ready, child."

As we walked the country road in the sunshine, me still on His shoulders, admiring the view, He continued, "Now might be a good time to forgive the boys for throwing snakes at you and causing you to fear."

Anxiousness, mixed with anger, started to rise inside me. An overwhelming urge to pull Jesus' hair came over me. He had walked me through much forgiveness, for things done to me that were much worse, so I was surprised at my reaction. The emotions kept rising and forced their way to the top, and like a child, I threw a fit.

"No! No! No!" I screamed at the top of my lungs. "I hate them! They're mean. They're bullies!"

Stunned at my own reaction and words, I sat on His shoulders afraid He would be mad at my outrage and put me down. He was not, and He did not. In my adult mind, I realized I had been holding those boys hostage in my heart. I could see each of their faces. They were standing as a group in a cage in my heart wanting to be let out; they did not want to be there. For years, I subconsciously kept them locked up wanting to see them punished. It never happened, and my anger stayed locked up with them.

I stood in my heart and stared at them for a long time. Finally deciding to forgive the boys, I marched my young-self over to the cage, opened it, and let them out. I told them I forgave them for being mean, for being bullies, for throwing snakes at me and causing me fear. Then I marched them over to Jesus. Justice was His to decide now, not mine. After the boys left my heart, I noticed a red ball of anger sitting inside the cage they had just vacated. I did not want the emotion tied to how they treated me anymore either, so I picked it up and handed it to Jesus. He gladly took it. When I asked Him to replace the anger with His love, He dismantled the cage and filled the space in my heart where the boys and the anger had once occupied with hundreds of tiny pink hearts full of love.

Lifting me back onto His shoulders, Jesus walked out of my heart and back up the driveway toward the house. Leaning down, I whispered. "I feel better now. I think I'm ready to try out my boots." Jesus swung me around and placed me on my own two feet. Together, we walked, hand-in-hand, the rest of the way to the house. When we got to the house, He sat outside in a lawn chair and watched as I ran and played in the yard unafraid. The five-year-old girl, with her snake-stomping boots, was finally able to run free as the little girl she was designed to be. Delighted, I ran over to Him and pulled Him out of the lawn chair. He laughed. We both laughed as we played together in the warm sunshine.

Jesus, in His love, had reframed my experience. What once had been a time locked with fear was now a memory of fun and joy, spending time with Jesus, running free, and feeling special with my brand new pair of boots. Boots Jesus had taken the time to custom make for me.

CHAPTER FOURTEEN

Bashing in the Face of Fear

Step by step, Jesus was gaining my trust and walking me through the rooms of my heart, clearing out debris and making beautiful the pieces of my life. The girl once bound by fear, performance, shame, and trauma was discovering how to live in freedom, love, hope, power, and relationship, all from a place of being loved.

Jesus' love was winning over fear, and I felt the hold of fear slipping from my shoulders with each passing day. So much so, that one day I realized fear no longer sat at the table. Fear was not even in the house, and I did not intend to invite fear back inside.

Fear wants to disrupt our peace and keep us from our destinies. Bible scholars point out that the Bible holds 365 instances of "fear not" or "do not be afraid"— a reminder for each day of the year against the persuasive force of fear. Fear circles relentlessly, looking for a path of least resistance. An entry point. An open door. An open window.

One day Fear himself showed up in a dream.

During this season in life, my family and I were praying and contending for the life of a family member. My dad and I felt it was a spiritual attack and I felt like the enemy was continuously trying to sneak up from behind, assaulting on all sides. It had been going on for months. I was weary, and I started to question if God had my back.

The dream that night was fraught with chaos. It was dark outside, and I could hear bugs hitting the window on the outside of the house. As I walked into a sitting room, I noticed an open window. The curtains were blowing, and a man in a yellow hat was climbing in through the window. I could not see his face, but I could feel the waves of fear radiating from him and rolling over me. Fear flooded my chest. Fear had found a way back inside. I awoke yelling for help. I prayed. My husband prayed. We both prayed until the fear lifted and I drifted back to sleep, safe in my husband's arms.

When I fell asleep, I found myself back in the dream. This time, however, Jesus was in the sitting room with His foot firmly planted on the back of the intruder who now lay face down on the floor. Jesus was holding a dark, wooden, baseball bat. Engraved down its side were the words in all caps: BE STRONG AND OF GOOD COURAGE. I'VE GOT YOUR BAT.

In my spirit, I knew He was telling me, "I'VE GOT YOUR BACK." Jesus jerked the intruder up and turned him around to face me. I did not recognize him. No one would. His face, grotesquely deformed, looked as if someone had beaten it to a pulp, beyond recognition, time and time again. Jesus handed me the bat.

The softer, sensitive side of me would like to tell you that I declined the bat, but I did not. I thanked Jesus for the bat, told Him I was sorry for doubting that He had my back, and set about pounding Fear's face myself. Holding nothing back, I hit Fear un-bottling all my emotion. When I was done, Jesus called an angel into the room who zip-tied Fear's hands behind his back. Jesus reached over and took a contract out of Fear's pocket and told him, "I'll see you in court."

Jesus and I talked about that dream for weeks!

When I asked Jesus about the contract, He shared that a contract, or an assignment, from the enemy, had been sent out to use fear to intimidate me. Jesus shared that when I had doubted, I opened a window a crack. That was all Fear needed. He had known about my doubt, about my fear that God did not have my back, and used the opportunity to sneak back inside.

I had so much to learn! Jesus went on to share that where He was taking me and what He was going to ask me to do with Him would require great courage and trust in Him. It would hold no room for Fear. Doubt was something I had to be especially mindful of as it was an entry point of which the enemy would take advantage every chance he could. Jesus shared the importance of guarding my heart and protecting my thoughts; the importance of being careful not to agree with the lies and half-truths the enemy continually tried to get me to believe.[6]

Since the beginning of time, satan has tried to get us to doubt our identity and to question God. He did it in the garden with Adam and Eve; he did it to Jesus when he tempted Him. His tactics have not changed. Satan is an expert at fear and intimidation. If he can use fear to immobilize us, we will not move forward. If we are caught up in self-doubt, we will circle the drain of confusion and end up in a pool of anxiousness, unable to function. Satan wants to keep us stuck in the mire of fear and confusion when we belong next to Jesus, living in freedom and having adventures with Him.

When I thanked Jesus for beating up Fear before I arrived, He laughed. "That wasn't me. That was us. That has been going on for the past ten years. Each time, you choose to trust Me and say no to Fear, it is a bash to his face."

Does Fear still circle the house? Yes. Does Fear still occasionally sneak inside? Yes, Fear is persistent, but when I realize he is hiding out, I get out my bat. I talk to Jesus. I ask Jesus why he is there. Did I believe a lie? Did he sneak in on a hurtful word or action by someone or even myself? Did he sneak in on a traumatic event? Did I open a window of doubt by not trusting God in some way?

When Jesus highlights the reason, if I need to *forgive* someone, I do; sometimes it is myself. I *repent* for agreeing with any lie, and then I *ask Jesus to tell me the truth,* the beautiful truth, my new truth, from the Source of Truth. I look for a verse from scripture to go with it, and I write the truth in my journal, on my mirror, on my heart, and in my mind. I plaster it to the window of my emotions. It is the first thing that Fear sees when he comes snooping back around. My favorite truth...

> *The Spirit of God in me is greater than fear. I am not timid, and with His Spirit, I have power, love, and a sound mind. (Reference 2 Timothy 1:7)*

For me, fear and worry walk in when I am not trusting Jesus in some area of my life. Jesus has led me through seasons of trusting Him to protect me, my family, my health, my finances, and the list goes on.

Over the past ten years, Jesus has continued to ask me the same question in different ways.

"Do you trust Me?"

The process of getting from my honest "no" to my honest "yes" has sometimes been hard and uncomfortable; however, it has always been worth it. Through the process, I have learned more about Jesus' heart and His great love. As I let Him heal and bring restoration to my life, He has filled those areas with His perfect love, the perfect love that casts out fear: fear of being punished, fear of being abandoned, fear of being rejected, fear of being unloved in my imperfections, and fear of Jesus not being there when I need Him.

> *There is no fear in love. But perfect love drives out fear because fear has to do with punishment. The one who fears is not made perfect in love (1 John 4:18).*

His perfect love bound up my broken heart and set this captive free. It healed me and released me into my true identity. His perfect love wants the same for you.

CHAPTER FIFTEEN

The Warrior Within

As Jesus taught me who I was in Him, I began to see myself differently than I had before. Gone was the fearful girl. Emerging was a warrior with new-found strength, one who would take a bat to the face of Fear. Who knew?

I was also learning more about the craftiness of satan and his dark angels, the demons. I knew firsthand the ones who had set up residence in my life throughout the years. Some had ridden in on the tails of past generations and trauma; others entered through the doors I propped open through actions of my own.

It took a while, and it was not easy, but I was intent on letting Jesus enter every room and clean out whatever did not belong. Jesus took care of some unholy spirits as He worked in rooms of my heart. Trained ministry teams helped to kick out other unwanted occupants.

As I climbed into bed one night, I asked Jesus to show me my authority in the kingdom. I knew He wanted me to share and release His love, but what about helping others find freedom? He answered with another dream.

Entering the dream mid-action, I found myself standing in a hallway. Demons lay on the ground around me defeated, beaten, still smoldering in their ashes. Apparently, I had been the cause of their demise. Satan appeared at the end of the hall as the red devil seen in movies. He stood for a few moments surveying the damage then confidently strode toward me. I knew he wanted to destroy me.

"I'm not afraid of you," I exclaimed boldly.

He tried to grab me, but I went low and grabbed his ankles. Then I proceeded to swing him around, like a figure skater swinging his partner by her feet in the infamous move called the Pamchenko, except I made sure his head hit the floor each time it came close to it. When he was unconscious from his head hitting the floor so many times, I threw him down and walked away.

Fear never entered my mind.

I woke up in awe. *That was me? Wow! I did not know I had that in me!* I began talking to Jesus, and He explained that the warrior was within me. I was designed to be on Jesus' side, and the Holy Spirit's power flowed within. I had been designed to help lead others into the arms of Jesus and help them find freedom and restoration, too. Having shown me my authority, I asked Jesus to teach me how to help others.

Jesus and the Holy Spirit led me to conferences and teachers who taught on inner healing and freedom. As the teaching unfolded, I realized Jesus and I had already walked through much of it together. I was gaining a deeper understanding of what I had experienced previously with Him.

I am blessed to be part of a church today that believes in physical and inner healing, deliverance, and that the gifts mentioned in First Corinthians chapter 12 exist today. I count it a great honor to help others find freedom and their personal identity in Jesus. One of my greatest joys is to lead individuals and groups into His Presence for when Jesus, the Lover of Our Souls, is brought into the picture, beautiful, life-change happens. My story and this book is a testament to Jesus' healing love. Part II will help you walk a path of healing and freedom of your own with Him.

Knowing Jesus as I know Him now, I am sometimes sad that I did not understand who He was sooner. Growing up the emphasis seemed to be more on what one "should" and "should not" do. A person should read the Bible, pray, and go to church. I saw these actions as rules to earn approval. Now I realize the "shoulds" are invitations and places where I can encounter His voice, His heart, and His love on a personal level. Whether I am digging for a treasure in the Scriptures, having a conversation with Jesus in my heart, going on an adventure with the Holy Spirit, or talking to Papa God about a need, I know I am loved and accepted regardless of what I do or do not do. I have experienced that love firsthand, and I know He is for me and wants the best for me. Jesus has all the answers, and when we take time to engage with Him,

He is happy to encourage us, speak life to us, advise us, and sing over us. He is Comforter, Hope, and the Author and Finisher of Our Faith. Without Jesus, we really have nothing to hold onto that is of any real value.

Why then are many of us afraid to encounter Jesus and Father God?

For me, I did not know there was more until I experienced Jesus' love later in life. Yes, I was raised in the church. From the ages of five to twenty, I was present three times a week, but I was afraid of Father God. I did not trust Him thinking I continually disappointed Him and He wanted to punish me.

For you, it may be something different. Maybe others you saw as Christians hurt or disappointed you, maybe you are mad at God, or perhaps you are hanging expectations on the Trinity because of what you have experienced in your family. Perhaps you are ashamed of your past and do not think you will be accepted, or you are searching and trying different things, but have yet to encounter the One who can fill the empty void, lift the heaviness of depression, and lead you out of anxiousness to the still waters of peace. There is hope. Jesus' love can win over your actions, faulty beliefs, and struggles. I am thankful that His love won over my misbelief that it was about rules and performance. Your freedom and healing will not be found in religion, in rules, or whether you belong to a particular organization. It will be found in a Person, Jesus, through a personal relationship with Him.

Jesus is a safe place. He is the one person who will never give up on you or quit loving you. He is patient and never sees you as an outcast or mistake. Jesus' love on the cross shouts you are someone worth dying to save—someone worth rescuing, someone worth healing, someone worth redeeming, and someone who has a brave warrior within.

CHAPTER SIXTEEN

Follow the Way of Love

February 14, another Valentine's Day. A wave of sadness hit me, just as it had every Valentine's Day since Grandma stepped into Heaven fifteen years earlier after losing the battle with ovarian cancer.

I loved spending time with her. Creative and gifted with her hands, she painted, quilted, and made a living designing and sewing drapes. Growing up, my family and I would visit and pick blackberries growing along her back fence. Afterward, I sat on cushions on the floor of her living room and admired the many original paintings that hung across the wall. During her illness, she gave me one I had always admired. That bouquet of white daisies hangs in my bedroom in her honor.

Each of her quilts was unique and assembled with much thought and care. She made my husband and me a quilt as a wedding present and made special quilts for our sons when they were born. Grandma insisted that we use them and not store them; she wanted us to be wrapped in her love. She was a survivor like me, in a sense, but she did not physically win the war that ravaged her fragile body.

Grandma had a hard life, leaving a marriage with a lot of anger and little love. Maybe that was why she read romance novels all the time. She could escape reality as she sailed through the pages of someone else's love story or perhaps she was drawn to them, like so many others, because we are designed by our Creator to be cared for and loved.

On her last New Year's Eve, I sat by her bed. She asked me to make sure I would do something she thought she could ignore without consequences:

get a yearly exam, regardless of my age. She had not had one in years. If she had, doctors might have caught the cancer sooner giving her more time on earth.

Letting my mind drift back, I recalled her last days on earth. It was the day before my birthday, January 30, and I had traveled home to see her. She was unresponsive and had not opened her eyes in days. I was upset; I had not told her goodbye! I awoke the next morning with a prayer that, before I left, she would realize that I was by her side. I walked into her bedroom and gently kissed her. As my lips brushed her forehead, she opened her eyes and smiled. Looking directly into my eyes with eyes as bright as a child's, she exclaimed with a crystal clear voice, "There you are my angel!" Closing her eyes, she drifted back to sleep. That was the last time on earth I would gaze into my grandma's eyes or hear her voice. What a beautiful gift she and God gave me on the last birthday I would have with her. Tears, mixing with thankfulness and sorrow, flowed as I embarked on my journey home.

Each morning I called my parents for an update. Grandma was still on earth, although they were not sure why she kept hanging on. Deep inside, I knew. She would step into Heaven on Valentine's Day. What better day to go to God, who was love and who would love her completely. Somehow that brought me comfort. It was the perfect day to end her final chapter here on earth.

She stepped into Heaven February 14.

Every Valentine's Day since emotions of grief and sadness from losing her resurfaced. I wanted to celebrate Valentine's Day with my husband with a happy heart. Pulling a blanket up over me, I closed my eyes and prayed for Jesus to take away the grief and sadness that surfaced every Valentine holiday and replace it with His love.

Somewhere between consciousness and sleep, I found myself standing on a stage where one would perform a play. No people were in the audience, and the building seemed deserted. Turning around, I noticed light filtering from between the slight opening of the two heavy velvet drapes hanging across the back of the stage. Parting the drapes with my hands, I was met with a vividly stunning scene as fields of colorful flowers embraced the rolling countryside before me. I stepped through the heavy drapes onto a dirt path.

As I followed the path, I took my time admiring the colors and flowers bathed in light. I stopped in surprise. In a garden, was my grandma! A beautiful, light gold dress glistening with hundreds of tiny diamonds adorned her body. My eyes instinctively searched for Jesus. He was nearby, sitting on a bench, smiling. I walked over and sat next to Him.

"You can go talk to her," He said with a grin.

I hesitated, then stood up and ran through the garden gate. I found Grandma picking blackberries, and I wondered if she was making her famous blackberry pies for Jesus. She was beautiful and smiling at me as if she knew I was coming for a visit that day. I stared at her again in amazement. I had never seen anyone who had gone on to Heaven in any of my other times with Jesus. Love and peace surrounded her.

It surrounded me.

She smiled again and pointed to the field of flowers behind her garden. I laughed with joy. There were thousands of daisies!

Turning to face me, she softly said, "I finally have it—love. I am loved completely here in Heaven. It is a love I never experienced on earth!"

Tears welled up in my eyes. I was so happy for her! I felt it, too, the love. I did not want to leave. Ever.

Glancing over to Jesus she continued. "He makes a point to come by and see me. We have spent quite a bit of time together, working on something special. It's for you."

I looked at Jesus in surprise. He motioned for me to come back and sit with Him. Grandma went inside her quaint stone cottage and brought out a large white gift box. Smiling, she rested it on my lap. I lifted the top off and gasped. Inside was the most beautiful quilt made of a material that I had never seen on earth. It reminded me of a luxurious, thick, white silk.

Grandma lifted it out so I could see the quilt in its entirety.

Delicately embroidered daisies adorned the edges. In the middle of the quilt a large crown was intricately stitched in gold. Scattered around the crown were tiny diamonds that matched the diamonds in Grandma's dress.

Gold letters made an archway over the top of the crown: FOLLOW THE WAY OF LOVE.

The custom quilt was breathtaking. I studied it carefully and looked up in awe. Jesus and Grandma had huge smiles on their faces. They had designed and made the quilt, together, for me! Feeling their love for me, tears of appreciation ran down my face. I did not know what to say.

"I think she likes it," Jesus said grinning at Grandma.

"Like it? I love it!" I exclaimed.

The three of us lay down on the soft grass, looking up at the bluest of blue skies. Jesus spread the quilt over us. It was soft and comforting. With Jesus on my right and Grandma on my left, I felt safe and secure. A sense of peace and happiness washed over me.

I gazed at Grandma in her glorified body. She was peaceful and happy. She was completely healthy and whole, completely loved by her Beloved. The three of us talked about the challenges of life, the goodness of God, and the reality of His love. I thanked them both for the quilt, and for the gift of that moment. I did not want to leave, but after a while, Jesus pulled me to my feet. Draping His arm across my shoulders, He began walking me back to where I had first entered.

"Thank you for trusting Me and giving Me full access to your heart." He continued, "You have let Me into every room and allowed My love to transform you. You are a beautiful carrier of My light and My love."

I could not imagine my life without Him! Before Jesus encountered me with His deep love, my life was full of strife, earning, proving, worry, anxiousness, and fear. Now, however, my life was full of His love, and I felt free and happy. I stopped and tightly hugged Him.

"I always want to be your love and light," I whispered.

Arriving back at the entrance, Jesus turned me to face Him. What He was about to say held great importance. "You will need to keep your focus. The enemy will try to distract you with his ways, his lies, and his schemes. Do not let your focus be on what he is doing. Keep your focus on Me and what I am doing."

I nodded with understanding and reiterated, "Keep my eyes on you."

He smiled. "Yes. Keep your eyes on Me."

He added, "I've given you some pretty big gifts to help others. Use the gifts to bring people to Me; bring them to Me so they, too, will experience my love and healing. Use the gifts to connect their hearts to mine."

I did not know what to say. *He* was my gift.

"I promise."

Tilting my chin up, He kissed my forehead, and with a finger pointed to my heart, "Use the gifts with love, from the heart of love I gave you."

I nodded.

He turned and walked back toward Grandma's cottage and gardens. With a parting wave, He shouted back one last reminder.

"Follow the way of love."

Follow the way of love and eagerly desire gifts of the Spirit, especially prophecy (1 Corinthians 14:1).

That Valentine's Day, Jesus went above and beyond taking away the sadness and giving me a new memory to hold onto in my heart. Now, when Valentine's Day comes around, I no longer feel sadness, but the love of Jesus and Grandma, and a reminder to follow the way of love.

CHAPTER SEVENTEEN

The Invitation

My friend, I invite you to follow the way of love. Jesus' perfect love heals, redeems, restores, and sets us free. It starts with an invitation. The Giver of Life, Hope, and Freedom is at the door of your heart.

Jesus is speaking softly, asking you to trust Him and His love for you. He is waiting to take your hand and guide you through the process of healing and restoration. He wants you to do more than just survive; He wants you to thrive.

Just as Jesus opened the door for me, I now open the door for you.

Will you accept His invitation?

You are worth it. You are worth all of His goodness, all of His time, and all of the suffering Jesus endured on the cross. Your journey will not be easy. Some of it may stir up pain as you walk through some unpleasant memories and do some heart-and-soul cleansing, but Jesus will be there *with you*.

Jesus believes in you. I believe in you. All of Heaven believes in you.

My journey will not look like yours, and yours will not look like mine. We are each uniquely created individuals with a personal story and experiences. Yet, we all have the same choice. We can stay stuck in the mire of past events and regrets, or we can open the door to the One who loves us more than anyone has or ever will. We can accept the invitation to trust Him. We can invite Him in. We can give Him our hearts, and let His love win.

PART II

Welcome to Your Healing Journey

CHAPTER EIGHTEEN

Introduction to Your Healing Journey

Jesus and I are thrilled you are here! You made a conscious choice to be brave and courageous and accepted the invitation to take one step closer to healing and freedom, one step farther into your purpose and destiny. We are so proud of you!

In Part II you will learn how God designed you and the importance of partnering with Jesus in this healing model. We will dive into some facts surrounding traumatic memories, the Pain-Processing Pathway, and how unprocessed pain affects the spirit, soul, and body. Along the way, you will read stories from others who have received healing using this model and walk through healing exercises of your own with Jesus.

I ask you not to skip around but go through the chapters and exercises in the order placed as they build one upon another. As you work your way through the exercises, you will find helpful instructions and tips to help you get the most out of each one.

Think of the chapters and exercises leading up to the trauma memory work at the end of Part II as a heart-and-soul cleanse, a detox that will help remove a lot of the excess toxins you have been carrying from wounds of the past. By the time you get to the trauma memory work, my prayer is that you will have cultivated a deeper relationship with Jesus, become more familiar with His gentle voice and ways, trusted and allowed Him into some of the painful places, and received measures of healing along with a deep infilling of His love and peace.

Jesus is all about relationships and cares deeply for you. He understands what you have been through and knows that healing takes time. It is a process—a journey of love and trust—and one not to be rushed. Permit yourself to go with Jesus at your own pace. You did not get to the state in which you are now all at once. The bulk of my healing journey was over a five year period. I pray that with the information and tools shared in this book, your inner healing journey will take less time. If it does not, that is perfectly fine; trust Jesus and His timing. His timing is perfect, and He knows what you can handle at any given moment. He knows the way into your heart and soul and what needs to occur in the exact order to bring complete healing and restoration.

During your healing journey, I encourage you to connect with Jesus each day. It is okay just to sit and talk with Him in the quietness of your heart. It is okay to be with Him and get to know Him without necessarily doing anything. He knows that with time comes trust and with trust comes the ability to let Him into the places you have been protecting from further hurt.

As you work your way through Part II, you will find places to journal your experiences with Jesus. These exercises are important and will help you get to the root of what you are internalizing and believing from an experience. You will more than likely use these exercises more than once, so I have created a Healing Journal Workbook to accompany this book. It follows the flow of the chapters and has additional copies of the exercises in each section. Looking back, I wish I had one place to capture everything Jesus was doing in my life in relation to my healing journey. I want the Healing Journal Workbook to be this for you. Write in it, mark it up, highlight it, date it, and use every section. Let it be part of your story and testimony—a testimony that shouts healing, redemption, and freedom.

Through my personal healing journey, and leading others through theirs, I have found that some things are worth being reminded of countless times.

1. You are uniquely created and have a unique journey with real personal experiences. Jesus knows everything about you and everything you have experienced in your life. Thus, your healing journey will be personal to you and Him.

2. You are not a project to Him. When you put your trust in Jesus, you become a child of God. You are part of His family, and He cares for you. Jesus will tend to your heart with great care because you are His beloved and you are precious to Him.

3. Your body, soul, and spirit are interconnected. Here on earth, it makes you a complete person. When one is affected, the other two are affected. I and many others received physical healing alongside emotional healing when Jesus replaced an untruth with His truth and healed and restored an area in our hearts and minds.

4. Just as you are created with physical senses—natural abilities to see, smell, taste, hear, and feel—you are also designed with spiritual senses. Spiritual senses allow you to connect with Jesus in a personal way. Through the Holy Spirit, you have the ability to see Jesus, hear His voice, and feel His love and peace.

5. Jesus is not bound by time. He can take you back to memories and show you where He is present in them. He can heal them, reveal untruths, and release His truth. He can cleanse neural pathways, remove triggers, and reframe memories so they no longer hold pain.

6. Jesus is love and never comes with shame or condemnation. He is glad to be with you and never talks down to you or makes you feel bad about yourself. Jesus wants you to know that He sees you, hears you, and understands what you are experiencing and feeling. He wants to be with you—every step of the way.

7. Jesus is gentle and will not steamroll His way through your painful memories and unprocessed pathways. He knows exactly where to go when and in what order to bring you healing and restoration in a way that will strengthen you and your relationship with Him. He knows the pace at which you can go and enjoys being with you whether you are actively moving forward or choosing to rest in His grace for a while.

8. There is no one "formula." Jesus created you, so He knows best how to engage with you and bring you healing. He may reveal things to you during your quiet time with Him, through information and exercises in this book, memory work, dreams, visions, Scripture, or through the help of trained ministry teams and professional therapists. How Jesus engages with you may be different than how He engages with someone else. He designed you in love and knows how to walk you through your past in love. You can trust Him to care for you and your well-being.

9. Jesus is relational and wants us to not only have a relationship with Him but also to have a healthy support system around us. I encourage you to seek out others who love Jesus and with whom you can safely share things and who will pray for you as you walk through your healing journey.

10. Jesus never wastes an experience. While the enemy uses pain to destroy you, when you give that pain to Jesus, He can heal it and use it to empower you. Your greatest pain can become your greatest victory, a powerful testament of His great love for you.

Before we jump into the chapters, I want to be upfront with you. Satan does not want you spending time with Jesus, nor does he want you on your healing journey—he fears whom you will become when you spend time with the One in whose image you are created. Spending time with Jesus is more than a choice you will have to make each day. It is a determination in your heart to not let anyone or life's circumstances become more valuable than your time with Him.

To keep you from spending time with Jesus, satan will throw distractions at you and tell you that you are too tired or emotionally spent. He will whisper in your ear that you are broken beyond repair, unworthy, unlovable, and many more lies to keep you out of Jesus' arms. Do not listen to the liar, the enemy of your soul. Slam the door in his face, surrender your heart and soul to Jesus, and speak aloud the following declaration. Say it several times a day, a hundred times if you must. Say it until both your heart and mind grab hold of it. Declare it aloud over yourself.

PRAYER OF DECLARATION

I am WORTHY. I am worth being rescued. I am worth receiving Jesus' love for me. I am worth being healed and made whole.

I am WANTED. Jesus and My Heavenly Father want me. I have a place in the Family. I am never alone and always accepted.

I am VALUED. I am too important to let the weight of someone else's actions weigh me down and keep me locked up in pain. I am too valuable to allow rooms of bitterness, rejection, abandonment, and fear take up space in my heart.

I am CHOSEN. Jesus gave His all so I can have His all. Through Jesus, I can have freedom from the things that are holding me back and keeping me from walking in my full identity and purpose.

I am a VICTOR. I am not defined by the hurts or mistakes of my past. Today, I choose to move forward and meet with the One who loves me and who is for me—the One who can restore my heart and release my destiny.

Okay, now you are ready. Let us move on and talk about how we are designed by God—spirit, soul, and body—and how unhealed wounds of the past can keep us from being fully who God created us to be.

CHAPTER NINETEEN

Divine Design in a Fallen World

O ur Creator loves us. From the beginning of time, God desired a family. When we give our hearts and lives to Jesus, Father God welcomes us into *His* family (Romans 8:15). We do not have to wait to go to Heaven after we die to spend time with Jesus and our Heavenly Father. Through the Holy Spirit, we can have a personal relationship with them while we are here on earth. When God designed us, He gave each of us a spirit, soul, and body. When we accept Jesus as our Lord and Savior, we receive the third Person of the Trinity—God's Holy Spirit—in our hearts. The Holy Spirit is the Spirit of Truth who brings wisdom and revelation to our hearts/spirits. He awakens our spiritual senses, helps us have a deeper relationship with Jesus and Father God, and empowers us to walk out our destiny.

> *I keep asking that the God of our Lord Jesus Christ, the glorious Father, may give you the Spirit of wisdom and revelation, so that you may know him better. I pray that the eyes of your heart may be enlightened in order that you may know the hope to which he has called you (Ephesians 1:17-18b).*

When God designed you, He put your identity (what you look like and your personality) along with your destiny (plan for your life) in your human spirit (Psalm 139:13-17). At the core of your spirit is a deep longing for unconditional love and belonging—a place that only the love of your Heavenly Father can fulfill (1 John 4).

God gave His children a choice to love Him back and be part of His family forever, so He created the soul with three parts—mind, will, and emotions. Your mind intellectually thinks and processes. You dream and imagine. Your mind is also home to your memories, beliefs, and habits. With your will, you make choices and decide to take action or not. Your emotions allow you to express how you feel on the inside.

Your spirit, soul, and body are interconnected. For example, when you accept Jesus as your Savior, your spirit awakens to the truth of who Jesus is and what He did to prepare the way for you to have an eternal relationship with your Heavenly Father. In your mind, you process what that means and use your will to choose to accept Him into your heart/spirit. With your mouth, you confess that He is Lord of your life (Romans 10:9), and the Holy Spirit comes into your heart/spirit to help you live as a child of God.

As another example of all three working together, through your spirit and by the Holy Spirit within you, you worship God in spirit and truth (John 4:24), but you decide to do so in your soul. Physically, you raise your hands in worship as you close your eyes and picture in your mind God in His throne room. The Holy Spirit may show you things on the screen of your imagination, or open the eyes of your spirit to show you things in the spirit realm (John 3:3). How God designed you is quite remarkable. You are truly a masterpiece, made in the image of your Divine Creator to have a personal relationship with Him.

Satan does not want you to have a relationship with your Heavenly Father and to worship the One True God. He is jealous of God and wants you to worship him and keep you bound in darkness. He does not want you living in your true identity or your authority as God's child. He plans before you are born to crush your human spirit, destroy your soul, and harm you physically. He does not play fair and tries to bring harm to you through physical, mental, and emotional abuse, rejection, abandonment, trauma, fear, and the list goes on. He comes at you from every angle he can. He knows that every hurtful word and action not processed into a place of healing leaves a wound of some kind on your entire being.

The thief comes only to steal and kill and destroy; I have come that they may have life, and have it to the full (John 10:10).

You and I are designed in the image of our Divine Creator, yet we live in a fallen world where we are affected by sin and surrounded by hurt people who hurt people. When we are wounded, we become inward focused on our pain, build walls of self-protection, keep Jesus and others out, and stay stuck in the past unable to move forward. To bring us into lasting healing the source of the pain needs to be uncovered, cleansed, and healed. Lies intertwined into our beliefs need to be uprooted, and truth planted in their place.

Jesus knows the depths of our pain and when invited in will gently work His way into our heart and soul revealing protective walls and wounded areas. Jesus does not want us isolated and in pain. He wants to walk through the pain with us and bring us into a place of healing and restoration. His heart is to redeem all the pain we have suffered.

You matter to Jesus and nothing in your life is insignificant or too great for Him to heal. He knows every hurtful word and action you have experienced. He knows the words that were spoken over you when you were in your mother's womb. He knows the glances you endured from others who made you feel like you did not belong. He knows every time someone betrayed your trust and broke your heart. He knows the words screamed at you, the blows dealt you, the respect torn from you, and the pain endured when someone treated you like property to be used or owned. He knows about every cut on your body, soul, and heart. He wants to heal and redeem it all and move you from "victim" to "victor."

Jesus knows who He created you to be; before you were affected by sin and the hurtful words and actions of others. He did not come to earth to just provide a way for you to enter God's family; He came to have an ongoing personal relationship with you built on love and trust. He desires to see your heart and soul fully restored and your destiny fully released.

My prayer for you as you move forward is that you will cherish every moment you spend with Jesus. I know He cherishes every moment with you. To get a better understanding of why we walk through our healing journey *with* Jesus, turn the page.

He is waiting for you.

CHAPTER TWENTY

Walking Through Your Healing Journey with Jesus

Of the Trinity—God the Father, God the Son (Jesus), and God the Spirit (the Holy Spirit)—Jesus is the one many of us are most comfortable relating to because He took on human form and experienced what we experience on earth. When God sent Jesus to earth to provide a way for us to once again have a face-to-face relationship with our Heavenly Father, Jesus came as the expressed nature of God, who is love (1 John 4:8).

> *The virgin will conceive and give birth to a son, and they will call him Immanuel which means "God with us"*
> *(Matthew 1:23).*

When Jesus was born, He had a spirit, a soul, and a body complete with physical and spiritual senses, just like you and I. Physically, He had a brain, nervous system, bones, muscles, blood, et cetera. He had a will and made choices. He had a mind that processed thoughts. He had an imagination, memories, and emotions. He had a personality and a life purpose, and He went through the same type of experiences that we go through today.

Throughout the New Testament of the Bible, the authors, inspired by the Holy Spirit, gave first-hand knowledge of the humanness of Jesus; humanness that He chose to experience so that He could redeem the human race and truly understand and empathize as He helps us through our own journey. Here are some highlights that reflect His body, soul, and spirit:

Jesus was born.

The Word became flesh and made His dwelling among us (John 1:14).

And she gave birth to her firstborn, a son. She wrapped Him in cloths and placed Him in a manger, because there was no guest room available for them (Luke 2:7).

He grew. He studied. He worked.

And Jesus grew in wisdom and stature, and in favor with God and man (Luke 2:52).

Isn't this the carpenter? Isn't this Mary's son...(Mark 6:3).

Jesus had physical needs and became hungry, tired, and thirsty.

After fasting forty days and forty nights, he was hungry (Matthew 4:2).

And Jesus, tired as He was from the journey, sat down by the well (John 4:6).

Knowing that everything had now been finished, and so that Scripture would be fulfilled, Jesus said, 'I am thirsty' (John 19:28).

He died a physical death.

. . . when he had said this, he breathed his last (Luke 23:46).

He had a body that people saw and felt.

Before death: *And the people all tried to touch him, because power was coming from him and healing them all (Luke 6:19).*

After resurrection: Look at my hands and my feet. It is I myself! Touch me and see; a ghost does not have flesh and bones, as you see I have (Luke 24:39).

Then he said to Thomas, "Put your finger here; see my hands. Reach out your hand and put it into my side. Stop doubting and believe" (John 20:27).

Jesus experienced sorrow.

When Jesus saw her weeping, and the Jews who had come along with her also weeping, He was deeply moved in spirit and troubled...Jesus wept (John 11:33, 35).

His soul and spirit were troubled.

Now my soul is troubled...(John 12:27).

Jesus was troubled in spirit and testified...(John 13:21).

He prayed with loud cries and tears.

During the days of Jesus' life on earth, he offered up prayers and petitions with fervent cries and tears (Hebrews 5:7).

He felt grief.

When Jesus heard what had happened (the death of His friend and relative, John the Baptist), He withdrew by boat privately to a solitary place (Matthew 14:13; emphasis added).

He had a human will, and made choices.

Going a little farther, He fell with His face to the ground and prayed, "My Father, if it is possible, may this cup be taken from me. Yet not as I will, but as you will" (Matthew 26:39).

For I have come down from heaven not to do my will but to do the will of him who sent me (John 6:38).

Jesus chose to experience it all, even to become sin Himself so He could be our Savior. Second Corinthians 5:21 says, *God made him who had no sin to be sin for us, so that in him we might become the righteousness of God.*

Jesus was no stranger to being mistreated. Isaiah 53:3-5 is a beautiful picture of His love for us and what He went through to rescue and redeem our hearts, our souls, and our bodies.

He was despised and rejected by mankind, a man of suffering, and familiar with pain.

Like one from whom people hide their faces he was despised, and we held him in low esteem. Surely he took up our pain and bore our suffering, yet we considered him punished by God, stricken by him, and afflicted. But he was pierced for our transgressions, he was crushed for our iniquities; the punishment that brought us peace was on him, and by his wounds we are healed.

We have each felt the sting of rejection and abandonment from others being absent at some time in our life. Jesus experienced it, too. His own people rejected him. He was abandoned by those He loved and to whom He had spent countless hours teaching. He was scorned, shamed, and spit upon. He was beaten though He did nothing to deserve such treatment. He was called names, shown disrespect, and ridiculed by those who should have honored Him. His heart was broken. He was falsely accused, found guilty, and put to death for the wrongdoings of others.

Are you beginning to understand why we walk through our healing journey *with* Jesus? He has suffered, too. He gets it. He gets us. We are not meant to do life without Him. He cares so much that He left Heaven for you and me, to share in our humanity so that by His death He could break the power of satan over us. He came to free us from slavery (Hebrews 2:14). He was the sinless One whom the Heavenly Father sent to bind up the brokenhearted (That's us.), to proclaim liberty to the captives (That's us.), and release from prison those who are bound (That's us.) (Isaiah 61:1).

If you have not yet decided to have a personal relationship with Jesus, I encourage you to open your heart today and invite Him into your life. When you ask Jesus into your heart as your Savior and Lord, He is faithful to forgive your sins and bring you into the arms of your Heavenly Father. You also receive the beautiful gift of the Holy Spirit; the Spirit of Truth who never leaves you and brings revelation and understanding to your heart, guides you, and helps you walk out your purpose and story here on earth.

Here is a prayer to help you take that step of faith.

PRAYER TO GIVE YOUR HEART & LIFE TO JESUS

Jesus, thank you that you love me just as I am. Thank you that you came and died on the cross for me! Thank you for taking on my sins and taking the punishment for my wrongdoings so I can be cleansed and righteous in the sight of God the Father.

Today, I give you my life and my heart to love and change from the inside out. I trust in you and what your love did on the cross for me. Thank you, Jesus, for opening the door and for bringing me into the arms of my perfect Heavenly Father.

I welcome your gift of the Holy Spirit and receive your love for me.

If you just invited Jesus into your heart and life, give testimony to it by writing in the date you became a child of God and share the great news with someone. We would love to celebrate with you too. Connect with us at SparklingBrooks.com and let us know you are now in God's family.

Today, (Date) _____, I became a Child of God.

When you are ready to begin walking your road of healing with Jesus, write the date and sign your name to mark the day you grabbed hold of the hand of Jesus, and asked Him to lead the way.

Today, (Date) _____, I am beginning my journey of healing with Jesus.

Signed (Your name) _____

In this chapter, we established why Jesus walks the journey *with* us. In the next, you will learn the importance of having an attuned personal relationship with Him in the Secret Place.

CHAPTER TWENTY-ONE

Attunement and the Secret Place

Have you ever been, or are you currently, in a relationship where you and the other person freely share your deepest thoughts and feelings? You perceive that the other person sees you, listens to you, empathizes with you, and understands your situation. That person is content to be in the moment with you—all without judging you and what you say or how you feel.

In these moments of sharing and caring, both yours and the other person's relational circuits are turned on, and you are "tuned in" to each other. You feel seen, heard, and understood without being judged. You feel safe—safe enough to let down your guard and trust the other person enough to get connected at a heart level. Therapists call this "attunement."[7] When you feel connected, the love center of your brain turns on, specific feel-good chemicals are released, and feelings of peace, love, and joy can flow.[8]

You and I are emotionally, physically, and spiritually designed to have attuned relationships. Our spirits long for attunement with our Heavenly Father and Jesus and our souls long for attunement with others around us. We are relational beings designed for life-giving relationships.

Having an attuned relationship where you feel safe with Jesus is essential. Until you feel safe with Him, seen by Him, heard by Him, and understood by Him without judgment, you will not be able to open up and share your heart with Him so that He can help you. It will be emotionally and physically impossible. When you feel unsafe and disconnected from a person, the opposite happens as when you feel safe and connected. Your body's survival system views "disconnection" as a threat and releases stress chemicals into your bloodstream that in turn shut down the reasoning center in your brain inhibiting your ability to share and receive.[9]

Jesus understands the importance of feeling safe with Him and being able to open our hearts. Until we feel safe with Jesus, we will not trust Him with our pain. Jesus is patient, kind, loving, and gentle. He knows what past experiences impacted you and your ability to trust. Jesus knew I did not trust Him and the reasons why; that is why He took time winning my trust. His relentless love and patience spoke volumes; I was worth the time and effort. For me, Jesus had to win my trust before He won my heart. Jesus' patient love wants to do the same for you.

Building trust and connection come from spending time with someone and coming to understand his or her true intentions in a safe place. That is why your first exercise will be establishing a safe place of attunement with Jesus and getting to know His heart for you. As you become more attuned with Jesus and trust Him with more of your heart, short moments with Him will hopefully turn into a way of life—a life that is continually abiding in Him (John 15:4). Do not be discouraged if you have not yet fully experienced attunement with Him, or have not been able to attune with Him for an extended time. You will have plenty of practice as we will start each exercise attuning with Jesus.

One of the fundamentals that help when attuning with Jesus is establishing a place where you feel safe. I call this my "Secret Place." It is a place I picture in my mind and heart reserved only for Jesus and me; a place of deep peace where we spend time together and where I return when I feel disconnected or stuck when walking through a traumatic memory. Our Secret Place is our place of connection, our place of attunement.

In this first exercise, you will practice establishing your Secret Place and inviting Jesus to spend time with you there. I am excited for you! Regardless of where you are physically in the natural realm, you can attune to Jesus within your spirit and experience Him through your spiritual senses, which by the way, are why you have them. Using your spiritual senses is not "New Age," they are part of your original design. When you and I surrender ourselves to the Holy Spirit, He can work through our spiritual senses and our imagination so that we can experience Jesus in the Secret Place—we can see Him, feel His Presence, and hear His voice.

> *These are the things God has revealed to us by his Spirit. The Spirit searches all things, even the deep things of God. For who knows a person's thoughts except their own spirit within them? In the same way, no one knows the thoughts of God except the Spirit of God. What we have received is not the spirit of the world, but the Spirit who is from God, so that we may understand what God has freely given us (1 Corinthians 2:10-12).*

Exercise: Getting Attuned with Jesus in the Secret Place

Time: 10-20 Minutes

Physical Place: A quiet place away from distractions

Materials: Journal or paper and pen or pencil

This first exercise is foundational and will help you meet Jesus in a personal way and better understand His heart for you. It will become your place of safety and peace reserved only for you and Him. It is where you will become accustomed to hearing His voice, feeling His love, and experiencing His Presence. It is where you will become attuned to the One who loves you unconditionally without judgment.

The exercise is broken down into three steps.

1. Establishing your Secret Place

2. Inviting Jesus to be there with you

3. Inviting Jesus to speak to you

The more times you encounter Jesus in your Secret Place, the easier it will become to meet with Him, see Him, and talk with Him. Think of your spiritual senses as muscles. Just like our physical muscles, the more we use them, the more developed and stronger they become. This exercise will help you develop and strengthen your spiritual senses.

If this type of exercise is new to you, here are some tips to help you settle in, quiet your mind, and get the most out of the experience.

- Go to a quiet place away from disruptions. If you have kids, it may be in your shower or bathtub (Hey, I've been there.), or while they are asleep.

- Unplug from social media and your cell phone. This is time set aside to focus on you and Jesus. Your relationship is worth the investment.

- Bring a blank piece of paper for miscellaneous thoughts that keep popping up—like all those "to do" items. Get them out of your head. You can go back and visit them later.

- Remember my pep talk in Part II's intro chapter? Meeting Jesus in the Secret Place is a determination in your heart. Do not let the enemy sidetrack you or whisper negative thoughts to you. He will try to get you to question why Jesus would want to meet with you. He may even try to make you feel guilty thinking you should be doing something else during the time. If this happens, pause and say your declaration aloud.

PRAYER OF DECLARATION

I am WORTHY. I am worth being rescued. I am worth receiving Jesus' love for me. I am worth being healed and made whole.

I am WANTED. Jesus and My Heavenly Father want me. I have a place in the Family. I am never alone and always accepted.

I am VALUED. I am too important to let the weight of someone else's actions weigh me down and keep me locked up in pain. I am too valuable to allow rooms of bitterness, rejection, abandonment, and fear take up space in my heart.

I am CHOSEN. Jesus gave His all so I can have His all. Through Jesus, I can have freedom from the things that are holding me back and keeping me from walking in my full identity and purpose.

I am a VICTOR. I am not defined by the hurts or mistakes of my past. Today, I choose to move forward and meet with the One who loves me and who is for me—the One who can restore my heart and release my destiny.

To help you see Jesus through the Holy Spirit, and not through the lens of hurts from the past, here is an opening prayer to begin your time.

OPENING PRAYER

Jesus, thank you for designing me in your likeness; I am wonderfully made. Today, I surrender to the Holy Spirit my spirit, soul, and body. I ask you to cleanse my physical and spiritual senses and attune them to you through the Holy Spirit.

Cleanse and purify my mind and imagination from all things that are not of you. Help me see and perceive clearly and help me dwell on that which is good and deserves praise—that which is true, noble, right, pure, lovely, and honorable. Help me dwell on you, your love for me, and your truth.

I surrender myself to you. Thank you for your Presence of Peace. I ask that you surround me with it now, and quiet all distractions. Guard my mind and heart as I go to the Secret Place to meet with you. Thank you, Jesus, for your goodness and your love for me.

It is time to bring back that child-like faith and use your spiritual senses and imagination Jesus gave you for something wonderful; you and Jesus are meant for each other.

1. Establishing your Secret Place

Begin by asking the Holy Spirit to help you choose your Secret Place.

Holy Spirit, help me choose my Secret Place to meet with Jesus...a place of peace and safety.

Visualize a place that brings you peace. It can be somewhere you enjoyed visiting as a child or a place you enjoy visiting now. Some people picture a beach at sunrise or sunset; others love the mountains. Some picture their grandparents' farm or cottage; some picture a place they saw in a photo or painting. Wherever it is, make sure it is a quiet, peaceful place where you feel safe and secure. You are going to spend a lot of time with Jesus in your

Secret Place, so having some chairs or a bench where you and Jesus can sit will be helpful.

Having trouble picturing a peaceful place where you have previously been? Use your imagination and design one. For example, you might imagine a beautiful lake: The sun is out, ducks are swimming around, and you can see a few clouds reflected in the water. By the edge of the lake under a shade tree is a wooden bench. Walking over you notice someone has engraved "Our Secret Place" in the bench.

Get the picture? Once you have your Secret Place in your mind, spend some time in your Secret Place absorbing the peace around you. Sit down, get comfortable, and breathe in the fresh air. As you take deep breaths, inhale peace and exhale the tension you are carrying in your body. Permit yourself to relax. As you relax, look around and take in the beauty and scenery around you. Take a few minutes to journal.

Where is your Secret Place?

Describe or draw it in as much detail as you are able...

Explain how you are feeling physically and emotionally...

Remember, your Secret Place must be a place of peace where you feel safe.

Before we invite Jesus into the Secret Place, I want to share what Jesus is like and what He is not like. Jesus is love, truth, light, hope, grace, mercy, comfort, healing, redemption, restoration, and many more positive attributes wrapped up in one. He never condemns or makes you feel bad. Not once in my healing journey did Jesus make me feel *less than* or question whether I was worth loving. Not once did He tell me I disappointed Him. Those thoughts and feelings of unworthiness are what He came to reveal, heal, and correct.

Jesus reveals the truth and loves us into it.

The next part of this exercise is getting acquainted with the One who loves you just as you are—without judgments, shame, or condemnation. Jesus wants to spend time with you. He sees and hears you, and understands how hard things are for you. He is the One who can do something to help you; He is the One who can bring you peace.

2. Inviting Jesus to be there with you

Go to your Secret Place in your mind and sit in the peace. Ask the Holy Spirit to help you see Jesus in your mind and heart using your imagination and your spiritual eyes. When you are ready, invite Jesus into your Secret Place.

Holy Spirit, help me see Jesus in my mind and heart using my imagination and spiritual eyes. Jesus, I invite you to join me in our Secret Place.

Be open to how Jesus wants to appear to you. You may see Him walking toward you. You may feel His Presence beside you, a hand on your shoulder, or experience feelings of peace and love washing over you. Some people see or feel Him right away; for others, it takes time, especially if it is the first time inviting Him. Sit and enjoy the peace while you are waiting for Him to join you. When He arrives, enjoy His Presence and spend time just being with Him. Stay connected to His Presence and peace as long as possible, then take some time to journal.

How does Jesus come to you?

What does Jesus look like to you?

What are you experiencing physically and emotionally?

If you feel peace but do not easily experience seeing Jesus in your heart and mind, do not be discouraged. Some have experienced seeing Him within a few moments; for others, it has taken days or weeks of sitting in the peace of the Secret Place inviting Him, and waiting. Jesus is worth the wait. One of my friends shared that she felt a profound peace in her Secret Place. It was weeks before she saw Jesus, and when she did see Him, she realized that the peace she was experiencing *was* Him. He had been there all along; she just had not been able to visualize or see Him before that moment.

3. Inviting Jesus to speak to you

We entertain a lot of different voices in our minds; we have our thoughts, the opinions of others, and the whispers and lies of the enemy. In the Secret Place, you will practice "tuning" into the voice of Jesus in your heart and mind through the Holy Spirit using your spiritual ears. Jesus tells us in John 10:27 that those that follow Him listen to (hear) His voice and follow Him. Jesus' words of truth bring light and life to our hearts and souls. When we grasp the truth and agree with what Jesus says to us in our hearts, we think and act out the truth of what He says.

> *So then faith comes by hearing, and hearing by the word of God (Romans 10:17).*

*Do not conform to the pattern of this world, but be trans-
formed by the renewing of your mind. Then you will be able
to test and approve what God's will is--his good, pleasing and
perfect will (Romans 12:2).*

When Jesus speaks to you, it will be in love. He will never talk to you
in a way that shames or condemns. He thinks the best of you and wants to
help you.

Continue sitting in your peaceful Secret Place with Jesus. When you
are ready, invite the Holy Spirit to attune your spiritual ears to the voice of
Jesus and ask Jesus what it is He wants to tell you today.

**Holy Spirit, please attune my spiritual ears to hear the voice of Jesus
clearly and help me hear what Jesus is saying in my heart and mind.
Jesus, thank you for being with me in the Secret Place; what do you want
to tell me right now?**

What does Jesus say to you?

How do you feel about what He said?

What are you experiencing physically and emotionally?

Take some time reflecting on the words Jesus spoke. I encourage you
to look in your Bible and ask the Holy Spirit to highlight a verse of Scripture
to accompany the theme of what Jesus shared. For instance, if Jesus told you,
"You are beautiful to Me," you may want to write out Song of Solomon 2:10.

My beloved spoke and said to me, "Arise, my darling, my beautiful one, come with me."

Maybe Jesus spoke the words, "I know the sadness in your heart," Psalm 56:8 (NLT) may be a verse you want to write.

You keep track of all my sorrows. You have collected all my tears in your bottle. You have recorded each one in your book.

In the Healing Journal Workbook, you will find this flow simplified into one piece as well as additional copies of the exercise. I pray that your Secret Place with Jesus helps you connect with Him heart-to-heart as you begin to experience His love for you in profound ways. You may spend days in this one exercise getting to know Jesus safely. He understands. Take your time. When He knows you are ready, He will take your hand and invite you to take the next step.

He may even ask, "Do you trust Me?"

CHAPTER TWENTY-TWO

Created for Connection

In the previous chapter, I shared how God designed us for connected relationships where we feel safe, secure and loved. Attuned, heart-to-heart, we can open our hearts to share and receive. There are times, however, that we do not experience heart-to-heart connections. During those times of disconnectedness, we can think no one cares, and a feeling of loneliness settles into our soul. Deep down, a part of our heart and soul still longs for love and a sense of belonging.

One of my favorite books of the Bible is the Book of Psalms. Throughout the chapters, David, in his honest vulnerability, bares his heart and soul. Sometimes he feels safe and connected to God and other times he feels disconnected, abandoned, forgotten, and alone. Psalm 13:2 is a picture of one of those times.

> *How long, Lord?*
> *Will you forget me forever?*
> *How long will you hide your face from me?*
> *How long must I wrestle with my thoughts and day after day*
> *have sorrow in my heart?*

As the apostle Paul points out in Acts 13:22, David was a man after God's own heart, yet at times, even David felt disconnected from God and others. During those times, David did what we all do when we feel disconnected: we wrestle with our thoughts, trying to find a way back into a place of connectedness and peace, longing for attunement with someone who cares.

Designed for connection with God, you and I were connected to Him before we were born. Before our conception, God, in His love, wanted us and designed us to live a life full of love and purpose. In Jeremiah 1:5 God points out to Jeremiah, "Before I formed you in the womb I knew you, before you were born I set you apart..."

In God's appointed time, you and I are conceived and nestled deep inside our mother's womb. As we grow and develop inside of her, we hear her heartbeat and become familiar with her voice. In healthy and loving environments, we are safe and protected. We are loved and wanted. Then the moment comes when we leave our warm cocoon of safety and enter the cold world. We cannot rationalize what just happened, but the safety of our mother's womb is gone, and when that umbilical cord is cut, we are physically disconnected as well. Our cry is to be *reconnected* to our source of safety and comfort.

When my first son made his appearance into this world, he was in distress from a long labor and complications during the delivery process. Eventually responding to the medical team's efforts, he started to cry, and once those lungs started working, not one person on the medical team could comfort or calm him. His distressful cry continued until a nurse brought him to me. As he lay on my chest, skin-to-skin, listening to my voice, and feeling the familiar rhythm of my heartbeat under his small head, he began to subconsciously recognize I was his familiar place of love, safety, and peace. The tension dissolved from his tight tiny body, and his crying subsided. He soon drifted off to sleep, relaxed, in the comfort of my arms, reconnected to his source of comfort.

However, not everyone is able to experience a time of connection with one's birth mother. Due to life circumstances, some mothers have made the courageous and hard choice of letting someone else raise their precious son or daughter. I have friends who have the joy of adopting children into their families. I have other friends who do not know their birth parents and others who were placed in foster care because a parent was unable to care for them. Each person, at some time or another, wrestled with the *why* in which thoughts of being abandoned, unwanted, rejected, or unloved surfaced to the top. Whether or not they had a positive relationship with those who later raised them, there was the question of "Why did the one who carried me and gave birth to me choose to disconnect from me?" It is a natural question, one of which many may not receive the answer.

If this rings true for you, your feelings are valid. The connection that was supposed to take place between you and your birth mother did not occur. God, who knows your life's circumstances, provided a way for a connection between Him and you before you were born. He wanted you in His family. He says you are worthy. You are wanted. He has never abandoned you. He has always loved you and watched over you. You are never *less than* to Him.

You are more than what others or your circumstances say.

Look at David, the one-time shepherd boy whom God chose to anoint as King of Israel. The odds were against him from birth. He was conceived in secret when his father Jesse slept with someone other than his wife. One wonders what David felt and thought during those years, being the son of another mother. When he was young, David was sent out to the field, away from the others, out of sight, to watch over lowly sheep. He could have felt sorry for himself, and maybe he did for a while. He most likely heard time and time again whispers from others as well as satan...

You're not wanted.

You don't belong.

You aren't loveable.

You'll never amount to anything.

You're only good enough to hold a lowly job.

Have you heard those lies also? That is what they are—lies. Lies from the enemy as a tactic to keep you disconnected from God and others. Please do not listen to the lies any longer. God's heart is turned toward you. He loves you, and His greatest desire is for you to experience His love as a chosen son or daughter. Just like David, God has a plan to silence those voices inside your head and turn what you think is impossible into "more than" you can ever dream or imagine (Ephesians 3:20). When we open our hearts to our Heavenly Father and allow Him space to tell us who we are to Him and share with us whom He created us to be, regardless of circumstances or current understanding, we allow Him room to fill us with His love and with His peace that passes all understanding.

In spite of the circumstances surrounding his birth and family dynamics, David cultivated a heart connection with his Heavenly Father, God Himself. Even though he may have felt disconnected at times, such as in Psalm 13, David's heart always brought him back to his Heavenly Father and His love and acceptance of him. David penned these words as recorded in Psalm 139:13-18.

> *For you created my inmost being; you knit me together in my mother's womb. I praise you because I am fearfully and wonderfully made; your works are wonderful, I know that full well.*

> *My frame was not hidden from you when I was made in the secret place, when I was woven together in the depths of the earth. Your eyes saw my unformed body; all the days ordained for me were written in your book before one of them came to be. How amazing are your thoughts concerning me. How vast is the sum of them! Were I to count them, they would outnumber the grains of sand—when I awake, I am still with you.*

When our hearts connect to God's heart, it will not matter what others think of us or our current capabilities. God will make a way to fulfill His purposes in our lives as He did for David—despite life's circumstances.

While David was yet in the field coming to understand his identity in the Father, God set in motion plans for the prophet Samuel to anoint the next King of Israel. God instructed Samuel to go to Bethlehem because God had chosen one of Jesse's sons. First Samuel chapter 16 tells the story:

> *I have come to sacrifice to the Lord. Consecrate yourselves and come to the sacrifice with me. Then he (Samuel) consecrated Jesse and his sons and invited them to the sacrifice. When they arrived, Samuel saw Eliab and thought, Surely the Lord's anointed stands here before the Lord. But the Lord said to Samuel, "Do not consider his appearance or his height, for I have rejected him. The Lord does not look at the things people look at. People look at the outward appearance, but the Lord looks at the heart."*

God needed a specific person for a specific purpose, and He was determined to fulfill His purpose with someone who had a heart connection with Him. None of Jesse's seven sons presented to Samuel were the one. I wonder why, at that time, Jesse did not jump up and shout, "Wait, I have one more son!" Who would not be proud of a son that God Himself had hand-picked? Maybe Jesse was bound in his self-guilt and shame, embarrassed that he bore a son out of wedlock. I do not know, but it was not until Samuel questioned if these were all Jesse's sons that Jesse said there was one more—the youngest who was tending sheep. His father did not even offer to get David. Samuel told him to do so. David came, and in the powerful act of anointing, with his father and brothers present—despite Jesse's actions and family dynamics—God recognized and honored David's place in Jesse's family.

> *So Samuel took the horn of oil and anointed him in the presence of his brothers...(1 Samuel 16:13a).*

I love what David did after Samuel anointed him to be the next king. He returned to the field. He returned to talk to his Heavenly Father. Can you imagine how his thoughts toward himself changed from that day forward? God was training David in the field for a higher purpose; gaining his trust, building his character, and helping David understand His heart's intentions—despite the circumstances.

In the field, David learned the heart of His Heavenly Father. In the field, he learned how to protect, become a warrior, lead, and shepherd. After the anointing, David learned how to work with the Spirit of the Lord.

> *. . . and from that day on the Spirit of the Lord came powerfully upon David (1 Samuel 16:13b).*

Each moment in the field was valuable. It was foundational as it developed David for his future assignments with God. From the shepherd's field to King Saul's courts, to the battlefield, to the king of one tribe, to the king of a nation, God was *with* him. David's time in the field taught and honed the skills needed to fulfill what God had planned in David's story. Each place and each chapter brought new insight into God's nature and faithfulness as David became more refined for future roles.

Friend, never discount your past, your current circumstances, or your future. God never wastes an experience. When we give Jesus our feelings of abandonment, rejection, and loneliness, He can walk us through the journey of healing and restoration. When we allow Jesus' love to fill the holes in our hearts left from the choices of others to disconnect from us, we can walk with confidence into our purpose—fully loved, fully accepted, and fully alive—regardless of the situation that once left the deficit.

Jesus can take what you and I once considered questionable chapters in our lives and rewrite them into something beautiful. He did that for my friend Tina.

Tina loves the parents who adopted her and has a solid relationship with them, yet grew up feeling disconnected and lonely. One day she asked Jesus to show her why she was feeling that way. Little did she know, He was about to take her back to the very beginning.

All of my life I felt like I didn't belong. I felt unworthy of love and was sensitive to any rejection. I carried so much self-shame inside of me and felt unlovable. As a result, relationships were superficial because I didn't know how to connect to share love. I would mask the emptiness by projecting laughter on the exterior while lonely and hollow on the inside. You know the saying, "Fake it until you make it." Well, I was tired of faking it. I asked Jesus for help, and He led me to a Christian therapist. During one of the sessions, we asked Jesus to take me back to where my feelings of not belonging and feeling unworthy first started.

The memory He took me back to was when I was in my mother's womb! I was alone in darkness and saw nothing. I also felt nothing...no love, no joy, no sadness. I was completely void of any emotion. Suddenly I felt Jesus' Presence, and with His Presence came a feeling of peace.

I soon heard a muffled voice. Jesus shared with me that the voice was my biological mother. I heard another voice filled with compassion that seemed directed at me, the developing baby. Jesus shared that this was the voice of my biological grandmother. She was convincing my birth mom to go full-term with her pregnancy and have me.

When Jesus shared this revelation, the dark womb suddenly turned to light, and a rush of air filled my lungs to the depth of my core as I sat on the sofa in my therapist's office. I felt that my Heavenly Father, God, breathed life and love into the very essence of my being. I received God's pure, unconditional love—heart, soul, and body.

Jesus shared that my birth mother was His vessel. He put me there. He knew me and loved me before conception. I'm my Heavenly Father's daughter. That day, I had a revelation of His love for me and my heart connected to His in a deep, personal way. Since that day, I've been able to experience more and more of His love for me. I feel like my heart is now in alignment with His heart. I am God's child, a member of Jesus' family. That I belong to such a noble lineage is profound.

Since that day, Jesus continues to bring waves of love into my heart and continues to heal in different ways and deeper measures. I'm so thankful Jesus took the self-condemnation that I had been carrying from birth into adulthood and replaced it with His unconditional love. I finally have a sense of belonging. I am lovable and wanted! I no longer feel like I have to perform or do things to be accepted and loved. My sense of loneliness is gone, and I'm now able to receive love from my family and friends too.

None of us have a perfect family, nor will we understand everything that happens to us. Our hearts, designed to connect with our Creator's heart, long for His pure, unconditional, fulfilling love.

Being a son or daughter of our Heavenly Father is the lifeline to a love that completes us.

Disconnection can occur as early as birth from not having a proper bonding experience. It can happen when a child's or teenager's mother or father walks away or is taken away by life's circumstances. It can occur when a caretaker cannot provide nurturing care or is emotionally unavailable. It can happen when those close to us disappoint us or are absent when we need them most.

What do we do with loneliness and other feelings that come from disconnection? The next exercise will help you attune with Jesus again in the Secret Place and give the feelings to Him. It will provide you with an opportunity to open your heart—even if only a crack—and do an exchange; an exchange of loneliness for His love, a love that brings with it a true sense of belonging.

Exercise: Exchanging Loneliness for Love

Time: 15-20 Minutes

Physical Place: A quiet place away from distractions

Materials: Journal or paper and pen or pencil

In the last exercise, you established your Secret Place and invited Jesus to be present with you there. When He came, you became acquainted with His Presence, and He spoke with you. This exercise will help you do that again and strengthen your relationship; remember, an attuned relationship is one where both hearts are open to share and receive. This exercise will help you share your feelings/emotions with Jesus and receive more of His love.

Start out with your opening prayer of surrender and cleansing, and then go to your Secret Place.

OPENING PRAYER

Jesus, thank you for designing me in your likeness; I am wonderfully made. Today, I surrender to the Holy Spirit my spirit, soul, and body. I ask you to cleanse my physical and spiritual senses and attune them to you through the Holy Spirit.

Cleanse and purify my mind and imagination from all things that are not of you. Help me see and perceive clearly and help me dwell on that which is good and deserves praise—that which is true, noble, right, pure, lovely, and honorable. Help me dwell on you, your love for me, and your truth.

I surrender myself to you. Thank you for your Presence of Peace. I ask that you surround me with it now, and quiet all distractions. Guard my mind and heart as I go to the Secret Place to meet with you. Thank you, Jesus, for your goodness and your love for me.

When you are comfortable in your Secret Place and feel peace, invite Jesus to join you.

Jesus, I invite you to join me in our Secret Place.

When Jesus arrives, enjoy His Presence and the love and peace He brings, then journal what you are experiencing with Jesus. Notice what Jesus is doing and listen for Him to tell you something. I know He is happy to be with you.

What does Jesus do?

What does Jesus say?

What are you feeling emotionally and physically?

When you sense His peace, think of a time someone was absent when you needed him or her to be there for you (like a parent, friend, or someone else you were counting on).

Who was not there for you when you needed him or her to be?

Picture the feeling or emotion of the loneliness you felt at the time in your hands.

What does your feeling of loneliness look like?

Let Jesus know you do not want to feel lonely anymore, and hand Him your loneliness.

Jesus, I don't want to feel lonely anymore. Today, I'm handing it to you.

See Jesus taking it from you.

What does Jesus do with the loneliness?

When you are done giving the feeling of loneliness to Jesus, ask Him to cleanse any area where the loneliness settled in your spirit, soul, and body and to fill those places with His love.

Jesus, thank you for taking the feeling of loneliness from me when (Write out who wasn't there.) _____ wasn't there for me.

I ask you to cleanse any area where the loneliness settled in my spirit, soul, and body and fill those places with your love.

Picture Jesus cleansing the areas and filling the places with His love.

Journal what you experienced (saw, felt, heard Him say, et cetera) during the cleansing and filling of His love...

Take some additional time to sit with Jesus, enjoying His peace and His Presence.

Journal your thoughts and what you are feeling...

Finish off your time with a prayer of thankfulness.

Jesus, you created me in love for a purpose. Each day of my life was recorded in your book and laid out before my life began. Continue to fill my heart with your love and open my mind to fully understand the magnitude of your unsurpassable love for me all the days of my life. Help me take comfort in the realization that you knew me before I was born. Your placement in the womb was temporary, while my life with you is eternal. Thank you for loving me first and continuing to love me each day.

As you go through your healing journey and are able to open the door of your heart wider, it is helpful to continue this exercise—giving Jesus the emotions from being disconnected from others and letting Him fill those places with His love and acceptance. The additional copies of this exercise in the Healing Journal Workbook will give you a place to do that.

You are loved, my friend.

You are loved.

CHAPTER TWENTY-THREE

Wired for Peace

Just as God created each of us for a heart-to-heart relationship with Him, we are also designed to live in peace. Adam and Eve enjoyed peace and harmony as they spent time in the Garden with their Heavenly Father. Can you picture the moment God breathed life into His first children?

> *Then the Lord God formed a man from the dust of the ground and breathed into his nostrils the breath of life, and the man became a living being (Genesis 2:7).*

God's face was the first thing Adam and Eve saw; their Father's face, their Creator's face, a face beaming with pride because they were *His* kids! I can imagine His heart swelling with love as they exhaled the breath He blew into them and said their first word, "Abba!" which means Daddy, Papa, Father. I can imagine that first hug, a place of safety and protection as they enjoyed an attuned heart-to-heart relationship with their Father.

They spent time with Him each day, sharing with Him what they had discovered in the Garden. Watching in wonder as plants grew up from the ground, they listened as their Father showed them how to tend them. In the cool of the evening, God shared His heart and thoughts with His children, and they shared theirs with Him. That is the scene I imagine happened before they acted on a choice that affected all of us; before they listened to the voice of the liar, satan, instead of their Father's voice of truth, before they let doubt creep in and questioned God's Word, before they acted in disobedience and cast themselves and the entire human race into sin, hardship, and painful consequences.

Oh, the peace lost in that moment.

Adam and Eve disobeyed and experienced the effects of sin and the loss of peace emotionally, spiritually, and physically. They felt emotions of regret, shame, and embarrassment. Realizing they were naked, they retreated, hid from God, and did their best to cover themselves. None of this surprised God. Knowing His kids would make wrong choices, He chose to move forward creating us believing free will and the voluntary decision to love and spend time with Him was worth it. Before the creation of the foundations of the world, He and Jesus had a plan to provide a path back to Him (Ephesians 1:20). The plan unfolded in sacrificial love: a love so great that Jesus would come to take on sins and punishments and provide covering by His atoning blood. I am thankful Jesus, who listened to the voice of His Father, voluntarily chose to lay His will down and do what was required. I am grateful He came to earth to rescue us, heal us, and restore us. I am thankful that He came to restore our heart-to-heart connection with our Heavenly Father. I am grateful He came to bring us peace.

> *Peace I leave with you;* **my peace I give you.** *I do not give to you as the world gives. Do not let your hearts be troubled and do not be afraid (John 14:27).*

> *And the peace of God, which transcends all understanding, will guard your hearts and your minds in Christ Jesus (Philippians 4:7).*

Jesus' peace is the peace we all long to have. Our spirits want peace. Our minds want peace. Our bodies want peace.

It is in a state of peace, balance, and harmony that we thrive and function at our best.

What happens when we experience an event that causes distress instead of peace and contradicts our feelings of love, connectedness, and safety? We instinctively try to resolve it and find our way back to our place of peace and well-being. Dr. Karl Lehman, Christian psychiatrist and a leader in the field of faith-based emotional healing, explains that when we experience negative and painful events in life, our minds start down the "Pain-Processing Pathway." To get down the pathway successfully and to correctly interpret the meaning of what happened, we need not only to be able to feel emotionally connected (attuned) with someone safe; we also need to be able to navigate the situation in a satisfying way. When we have the connection, safety, and skills to emotionally and cognitively process the experience in a healthy way, we are then able to glean additional knowledge, skills, empathy, and a better understanding that leads to a more fulfilling life. We are able to get back into a place of peace and well-being.

However, when we are not able to get through the Pain-Processing Pathway successfully because we have not been able to feel safe and connected with someone, and/or we have not been able to emotionally and cognitively process the experience in a healthy way, we are left with unresolved trauma that affects us regardless of how long ago it occurred or how minor or major an experience seemed at the time. Trauma can occur at any age; even a surprisingly small painful experience when one is young can bring lasting effects.[10]

Unresolved traumas with the feelings and emotions felt at the time do not just disappear. They are stored in our nonconscious minds as long-term, emotionally-charged memories. If not processed into a place of peace, these memories take a toll on our lives damaging relationships, keeping us stuck unable to move forward, and causing sickness and disease.

Dr. Caroline Leaf, who has been studying the brain and the science of thought for over thirty years, explains that traumatic memories get stored in the nonconscious mind as "toxic memory trees." When a traumatic memory is pulled up by the subconscious mind, the memory becomes malleable and vibrates, allowing for a redesign, a reframing. It wants to be reviewed, healed, and brought to a place of peace. If a person is unable to process the memory successfully or deliberately chooses to ignore it and suppress it, the traumatic memory becomes more powerful, more toxic, and more damaging.[11]

Here is a brief look at the roles the conscious, subconscious, and nonconscious mind play and how they work together.

Think of the nonconscious mind as a deep underground storage bunker storing all experiences since conception. It is full of energy and is always working. It is home to beliefs, habits, behaviors, and deep-seated emotions programmed and reinforced over time. Long-term memories, as well as the feelings and emotions of those memories, are stored here and do not rise into the conscious mind whenever they want. They only rise to the surface when triggered by the subconscious mind trying to make sense of an incoming experience. Information in the underground bunker is not bound by time or space. Jesus, who is also not bound by time or space, can bring up stored memories during a time of healing.

The subconscious mind, between your nonconscious and conscious mind, is in charge of recent memories and is in continuous contact with the nonconscious mind. The memories stored here are for quick recall, such as the name of a person you just met, and procedural memories, such as how to drive a car or brush your teeth. The subconscious mind takes the information coming in through the senses (sight, sound, smell, taste, touch) and works with the nonconscious mind to make sense of it all testing its validity according to a person's current perceptions. The nonconscious and subconscious parts of the mind are working behind the scenes without a person consciously being aware of what they are doing.

The conscious mind, on the other hand, is what a person is actually aware of at any given moment. When you are awake, it is awake. When you are asleep, it is asleep. With your conscious mind, you can focus on something specific, make conscious decisions (Hmm, what shall I wear today?), and visualize. It is with the conscious mind one can imagine new things not experienced before like your Secret Place with Jesus. It is also where the imagination can paint pictures of what could go wrong expending energy worrying over things that do not come to pass over eighty-five percent of the time.[12]

It is relevant to note that a person can use the imagination in one's conscious mind to think and visualize positive or negative experiences; when this occurs, the nonconscious mind believes that what was imagined was real and stores it as such; it cannot tell the difference between real events and those imagined.[13] Understanding how He created us, Father God shared wisdom in

Scripture for us to think and visualize that which is positive, pure, and praise-worthy helping us fill our minds with life-giving thoughts and experiences.

> *Finally, brothers and sisters, whatever is true, whatever is noble, whatever is right, whatever is pure, whatever is lovely, whatever is admirable--if anything is excellent or praisewor-thy--think about such things (Philippians 4:8).*

> *Now to him who is able to do immeasurably more than all we ask or imagine, according to his power that is at work within us (Ephesians 3:20).*

Triggering of Memories

As one experiences life, the five senses continuously bring in new infor-mation. As this is happening, the subconscious mind is looking for help from the nonconscious mind to make sense of it all; it needs help evaluating and processing the incoming data. *Has something similar occurred in the past? How did it make me feel? Was it a positive or negative experience? Am I safe or do I need to protect myself?*

The nonconscious mind searches its stored memories and starts send-ing, one at a time, five to seven memories that have similar data points, to be reviewed. An emotionally-charged memory usually gets more attention and is the one the subconscious most chooses to help evaluate the current situation. When a retrieved memory—along with its emotions, beliefs, thoughts, and behavior—come into focus, it becomes the lens through which one views the current experience. If the memory has undealt trauma the person finds him or herself reacting from the toxic emotions previously stored with the retrieved memory.[14]

Dr. Lehman points out that when something in the present causes our minds to open traumatic memories, unresolved content from the previous memories is activated. When this occurs, unprocessed physical sensations, unresolved negative emotions, feelings of inadequacy, confusion, and dis-torted interpretations come forward and *feel true in the present.*[15]

This process happens so fast a person most likely is not aware of the "trigger." One may be enjoying the day, then instantly feel scared, anxious, frustrated, angry, or sad. A person may go from contentment to fighting an urge to run, fight, or hide, finding oneself *reacting* in a way that the current situation does not warrant.

The power of a trigger can depend on how closely it resembles a past situation or relationship, the depth of the pain and trauma, and the state of the body and brain when the triggering occurs.[16] Our five senses play an active role in triggering painful and traumatic memories. It could be a faint smell of alcohol that was once on the breath of an abuser. It might be seeing bullying on TV, reminding of a time you were bullied in grade school. The sound of a slamming door could bring up emotions previously felt when a loved one slammed a door, left, and never returned. It might be yelling or similar hurtful words that cut your heart. It could be the smell or a taste of a particular food that once made you ill. It could even be a song playing on the radio as it once was for me...

It was a long trip, and I offered to drive for a while. I tuned the radio to a local radio station in the area and enjoyed the scenery rolling by. About an hour into the drive, a feeling of sadness welled up within me, and tears filled my eyes. Within moments, I had gone from feeling peaceful and admiring the scenery to feeling deep sadness and restraining tears. I told my husband what I was experiencing. Quietly, he pondered. Realization soon came, "It's the song on the radio...they played it at your mom's funeral."

He was right! The first and last time I heard that song was while I was sitting at her funeral, holding back tears. I was up next to speak and afraid if I let them out, I would become an emotional mess and be unable to fulfill my part in the service. When I heard the song almost two years later, the stored memory that included that song was retrieved bringing with it my feeling of sadness during that time. The driving or the scenery had not made me sad; it was the past emotion attached to something triggered; a song I heard almost two years beforehand.

When we returned home from our trip, I spent time processing with Jesus. He and I went back to the memory, and He showed me that He was there with me that day, sitting right next to me in the service with His arm around me. He told me it was okay to cry. Missing her was okay. It was okay to grieve. I did not have to hold it all in, so in the quietness of my study sitting in my favorite chair, I cried. I cried and cried and cried. I let out the loss and pain I had held in during her funeral. I let the tears cascade down my face until there were no more in that moment. Jesus held me through it all. When I was done releasing my tears and pain, He replaced the loss and sadness with His love—and with His peace.

A few months later, a friend randomly mentioned that song as being one of her favorites, and that she wanted it played one day at her funeral. Instead of sadness, I felt peace. Jesus had walked me along the Pain-Processing Pathway successfully. I felt connected to Him, it had been safe to grieve, and I had let go of the sadness I had been carrying since that moment at her funeral. Since I had finished processing the memory and was at a place of peace, the energy I previously used to suppress that traumatic memory was now being used to remember the beautiful reframed memory—a memory with me in the arms of Jesus being filled with more of His love and peace and an overwhelming sense of His nearness during a difficult time in my life.

Exercise: Revisiting a Memory | Exchanging Sadness for Peace

Time: 15-20 Minutes
Physical Place: A quiet place away from distractions
Materials: Journal or paper and pen or pencil

When God healed my neck, and I encountered His love in the depth of my heart, my view of Him shifted just enough to allow me to connect with Jesus. As I became acquainted with Jesus and trusted Him with more of my past, He took me back to painful, traumatic memories to heal them. Through the process of healing a traumatic memory, the memory was reframed. The structure of the memory itself changed; no longer was it a traumatic memory tree with dead branches full of negative emotions, it had structurally altered holding a memory that now blossomed with His Presence and peace.

In this exercise, you will practice going back to a memory with Jesus. You will also have the opportunity to journal what you were experiencing and what was going on around you during that time, which will help you identify its triggers. You will have an opportunity to give the emotion(s) to Jesus and ask Him to help you move into a place of peace. You will finish up by asking Him to cleanse the neural pathway of the original memory, remove triggers, and establish your new, reframed memory.

Once again, start with an opening prayer of surrender and cleansing.

OPENING PRAYER

Jesus, thank you for designing me in your likeness; I am wonderfully made. Today, I surrender to the Holy Spirit my spirit, soul, and body. I ask you to cleanse my physical and spiritual senses and attune them to you through the Holy Spirit.

Cleanse and purify my mind and imagination from all things that are not of you. Help me see and perceive clearly and help me dwell on that which is good and deserves praise—that which is true, noble, right, pure, lovely, and honorable. Help me dwell on you, your love for me, and your truth.

I surrender myself to you. Thank you for your Presence of Peace. I ask that you surround me with it now, and quiet all distractions. Guard my mind and heart as I go to the Secret Place to meet with you and as you take me to a memory. Thank you, Jesus, for your goodness and your love for me.

When you are in your Secret Place and feel peace, invite Jesus to join you.

Jesus, please join me in our Secret Place.

When Jesus joins you, enjoy His Presence and the love and additional peace that He brings. Notice what He is doing and journal anything He tells you. I know He is happy to be with you.

What does Jesus do?

What does Jesus say?

How do you feel emotionally and physically?

When ready, follow the prompts below and ask Jesus to bring to your conscious mind a memory where you felt sad. Then ask Jesus to go with you into that memory so you can see Him with you. If at any time, during the memory work, you look for Jesus and do not see Him or you feel uncomfortable, return to your Secret Place and talk with Jesus about it. You are on this journey *with* Jesus. He is your safe place in the memory, so it is essential to know He is with you during each piece of the exercise. If several memories rise, ask Jesus upon which memory He wants you to focus. We are using the emotion of sadness for this exercise, but if other emotions rise to the surface, follow the same flow and give the emotion(s) to Jesus along with the sadness.

Jesus, will you please take me back to a memory where I felt sad, and let me see where you are in it?

Where is Jesus in the memory?

What is Jesus doing?

Journal the memory asking Jesus to help you remember details that He wants you to remember. Write as much as you can remember to help you identify possible triggers.

Where did the memory take place?
For example: home, school, neighbors, et cetera...

At what age or at what time of life did the experience take place? For example: age 6, junior high, newly married, et cetera...

List specific people involved.
For example: neighbor, parent, friend, spouse, authority figure, et cetera...

What is happening in the memory?

What are you hearing, seeing, smelling, tasting, and experiencing physically?

List other emotions in addition to sadness you are feeling...

Jesus felt sadness, too, and understands how you feel. Talk with Jesus about the experience and what made you sad. Sometimes it helps to write things out, so I have given you a place to journal thoughts and further conversations with Him.

Journal your thoughts with Jesus about the experience...

During your conversation with Jesus, invite Him to share His heart with you about the experience.

Jesus, I thank you for being with me. Is there anything you want to show or tell me about this memory?

What does Jesus say or reveal to you about the experience and the sadness?

When you are ready, picture the sadness in your hands and let Jesus know you want to give Him the emotion of sadness in exchange for His peace and love.

Jesus, I don't want to carry this sadness from this experience anymore.

Picture the sadness in your hands and hand it to Jesus.

What does your feeling of sadness look like?

Jesus, I'm giving this sadness to you now.

See Jesus taking it from you.

What does Jesus do with the sadness?

Take a few moments and ask Jesus if there are any other emotions He wants you to give Him at this time. If there are, hand the additional emotions to Him.

Journal any other emotions you handed to Jesus...

When you are finished giving Jesus the sadness and any other emotions, ask Him to cleanse the areas where the emotions settled in your spirit, soul, and body and fill those areas with His love and peace.

Jesus, I thank you for taking the feeling of sadness that came with this memory. I ask you to cleanse any area in my spirit, soul, and body where the sadness settled and fill those places with your love and your peace.

Picture Jesus cleansing and filling those areas with His love and peace.

Journal anything you see or experience during this time...

Now, ask Jesus what He wants you to remember when you think about this experience. What is your reframed memory? For example, in my story about my mom's funeral, I remember Jesus sitting right next to me, holding me as I cried out my sadness in His arms and afterward Him filling me with His peace. Now when I think back, I remember Him holding me and I feel peace.

Thank you, Jesus, for taking my sadness and replacing it with your love and peace. What memory do you want me to remember now instead of the one with sadness?

What does Jesus show or tell you?

Now that you have given your sadness to Jesus and He has given you a new memory with Him in it, follow the prompts below asking Him to (1) wash out the old neural pathways that originally tied that memory with the emotion of sadness, (2) remove the triggers that were set up in the original memory, and (3) firmly establish your reframed memory—the one where you are now with Him experiencing His peace instead of sadness.

Jesus, I thank you for walking through this memory with me bringing it from a place of sadness into a place of peace.

Please cleanse the old neural pathways and remove any remaining traces of sadness. Remove all triggers set in place in the original experience, and firmly establish my reframed memory where you are with me.

Thank you for your healing grace and for taking my sadness and filling those places with your love and peace.

When you are finished, spend some quiet time with Jesus in your Secret Place soaking in more of His love and peace.

CHAPTER TWENTY-FOUR

Root Emotions of Love and Fear

Earlier we talked about how we are designed to have an attuned heart connection with Jesus and how God wired us for peace. We are also intrinsically designed and wired for love. We are created in love, to be loved, and to love God and others. Yes, that is a lot of love. God is love (1 John 4:8), and we are created in His likeness.

As we experience unconditional love from Jesus, we begin to understand His goodness and His heart's intent. As we realize that Jesus is a safe person who is with us, we start to trust Him with our hurts, and we give him access to our hearts and to our souls—souls that carry negative, toxic emotions from unprocessed trauma and wounding by others; souls that neurologically carry two powerful root emotions—love and fear. Dr. Leaf points out that the anatomy and physiology of love and fear go down to a molecular and genetic level; love and fear cannot co-exist. In any one moment, we either live from the root emotion of love or the root emotion of fear.

> *We are designed for love, yet we have learned and been conditioned to fear.*

When we have healthy connections with others, when perceived needs are met, and when we have positive experiences where we feel loved and secure, feel-good chemicals such as oxytocin and dopamine are released, giving us a sense of well-being. From that place of feeling loved, we experience joy, peace, happiness, patience, kindness, gentleness, self-control, compassion, calmness, inspiration, hope, excitement, and satisfaction. When we do not have healthy connections with others and have unresolved negative experiences, we feel fear and experience its emotional offshoots of hate, anger, bitterness, rage, irritation, unkindness, worry, self-pity, jealousy, obsession, and cynicism. [17]

God is love. As believers, we are one in Spirit with Him (1 Corinthians 6:17). However, until the soul and thoughts let go of fear and instead embrace His love in all areas of life, fear has a place, affecting the mind, emotions, and body. Scientific research shows that fear triggers more than 1,400 physical and chemical responses and activates more than thirty different hormones. Research also suggests that thoughts and fear-based emotions cause 75% to 95% of the illnesses that plague people today. [18]

Fear and its offshoots affect our entire well-being stealing peace of mind and causing stress to bodies. When disconnection takes place, our sense of safety in relation to others and ourselves is shaken, and when safety is threatened, the body's survival system activates launching a sequence of nerve-cell firings and chemical releases that prepare the body for running or fighting. The brain and nervous system turn into a rapid response team.

When the mind perceives distress, it sends out an SOS, and the sympathetic nervous system springs into action to help. To help access more light to see what is going on, the pupils dilate, and one becomes hyper-vigilant, instantly on high-alert, scanning for threats. To stay focused on surviving, the brain flips a switch and powers down the brain's frontal lobes' reasoning centers. Adrenaline, noradrenaline, and cortisol are released into the bloodstream. Blood pressure rises and heart rate increases. Blood is diverted from the digestive tract and sent to help the muscles and limbs; the body needs that energy to fight or run. Muscles tense and fear floods the body as the survival system slingshots into "fight or flight" mode. [19]

Our physical fight-or-flight survival system is a great system if we, like our ancestors, are in the occasional danger of being eaten by a wild animal. In today's world, however, we rarely find ourselves in a place of peace. Our survival system is more "on" than "off" due to disconnection from relationships, conflicts, a variety of stressful situations at home and work, and the ongoing triggering of unresolved traumatic memories.

The survival system becomes an unending cycle; emotional stressors are continuously present, and we constantly feel under attack; therefore, we are always on high-alert looking for threats and *expecting* the worst to happen. Our fight-or-flight survival system stays turned on, pumping out stress hormones, and we later find our adrenal glands overused and ourselves in a state of adrenal fatigue. Cortisol, the primary stress hormone, increases blood sugar levels, lowering the immune system, and suppressing the digestive and reproductive systems. These ongoing hormone stressors put us at an increased risk for a myriad of health problems including anxiety, depression, digestive problems, headaches, heart disease, sleep problems, weight gain, and memory and concentration impairment. [20]

Post-Traumatic Stress Disorder (PTSD) is not reserved only for those who have seen action in combat. It can occur with someone who has been involved in or witnessed a natural disaster, assault or abuse, a serious accident, or an emotional or physical loss. What one person may be able to process and emotionally handle, another person may not.[21] Here is a more in-depth look into trauma and the effects it can have on a person mentally, emotionally, and physically.

Memories show up unannounced and unwanted.

- Memories intrusively show up giving a person no control of when and if they are triggered.

- Flashbacks cause one to relive the traumatic event as if it was happening again in the present.

- Upsetting dreams or nightmares occur about the traumatic event.

When a person is not yet able to process a traumatic memory into a place of peace, one of the internal coping strategies is to try and avoid triggering it. A person may find one's self:

- Avoiding consciously thinking or talking about the traumatic event

- Avoiding places, activities, or people that remind him or her of the traumatic event

Since the memory is unresolved and stuck in the Pain-Processing Pathway, it contains negative thoughts and toxic emotions that affect a person's thinking and mood. A person may find one's self:

- Thinking negative thoughts about one's self, other people, or the world

- Feeling hopelessness about the future

- Having memory problems, including blocking out important aspects of the traumatic event

- Feeling detached from family and friends

- Losing interest in activities once enjoyed

- Finding it difficult to experience positive emotions

- Becoming emotionally numb

Other changes in physical and emotional reactions occur, and a person may find one's self:

- Easily startled or frightened

- Always on guard, looking for danger

- Having trouble sleeping and concentrating

- Feeling overwhelmed with guilt or shame

- Engaging in self-destructive behaviors, such as drinking too much or driving too fast

- Having outbursts of anger or irritability or other aggressive behavior

Post-trauma symptoms can affect anyone, can vary from person to person, and show up in varying degrees. They may show up immediately or years after an unresolved experience affecting relationships, performance at work, family life, and sometimes the ability to do normal daily tasks. [22]

Over time, we may find ways to self-regulate our stress through self-help books or relaxation focused strategies such as the following: [23]

- Walking, running, or swimming while repeating a positive word or phrase with each step or stroke

- Utilizing deep diaphragmatic breathing exercises, with a focus on the breath

- Repeating prayers or scriptures aloud, such as "The Lord is my Shepherd, I shall not want."

These valuable strategies help us cope, but our hearts, minds, and bodies yearn for healing and long for lasting peace. We want to live the abundant peace and joy-filled life Jesus came to give us. We are wired to live that way from birth, yet life happens, and the thief comes in and camps out on unprocessed trauma, stealing our peace and joy.

> *The thief comes only to steal and kill and destroy; I have come that they (That's you and me.) may have life, and have it to the full (John 10:10; emphasis added).*

We have a conscious choice to make. We can (1) allow ourselves to continue suffering, (2) learn to manage symptoms, or (3) seek help in walking through the Pain-Processing Pathway successfully. The exercises in this book will help you do that with Jesus. From personal experience, I can tell you that option one takes you deeper into despair and discouragement, while option two only gets you part way. Managing symptoms expends a lot of energy over the course of a lifetime, and as we age, the frontal lobes of our brains, the areas that help us reason and cope, become progressively weaker, requiring even more strength and energy to manage the symptoms and cope psychologically. [24]

We can try to decrease external stressors to help us manage better, but watch out when life throws a few extras. *Kaboom!* We can find ourselves with less patience, explosions of anger, and hurtful words directed at those around us. We can find ourselves reaching for our food, drink, or drug of choice. We can find ourselves at the end of our ropes, begging for someone to pull us back up to safety.

None of us travel through this broken world without having some degree of unresolved pain along the way, and we are most vulnerable during our early years. As children, we do not have control over what is happening around us or to us. We have powerful emotions, but not the skills to regulate them. Our imagination is highly active, and our reasoning center not fully developed. It is the time in life when we need love and safety the most, but we do not yet have the tools or resources to take care of ourselves or the capability to fight or run away. What do we do? We build walls of self-protection and find ways of coping so that we can adapt to and survive the world in which we live.

It is also the time in our lives when we form our strongest nonconscious beliefs. Through the study of brainwave frequencies, we know that from our time in the womb up to the age of five or six what we experience and learn from the environment goes *directly into our nonconscious mind*, laying down networks of memories, learned behaviors, and belief systems. During this time, we are learning from both positive and negative experiences that, in turn, cause us to develop behaviors and habits.[25]

For instance, my newborn son soon learned that when he cried because he was hungry, I would come and give him what he needed. It only took a few times of his crying, my coming, and his feeling cared for, to learn I was a source of comfort for him; he learned I fed him when he was hungry.

What happens when we cry out at a time when no one here on earth connects, cares for us, or comes to our rescue, such as the time when I was five crying out for my parents from the bathtub, only to be met with silence? I went from feeling safe and secure to being disconnected in that situation and feeling abandoned and unwanted. When Jesus later took me back to that memory, and He came into that memory and sat beside the bathtub so that I would not be alone, I had a connection—with Him. I felt safe because He was with me. His words assured me that He had not abandoned me, that I was not alone in the world, and that He would never leave me. I was experiencing attunement with Him.

During those moments of reframing the memory, I felt cared for, safe, seen, and heard. I felt secure and went from a place of fear to a place of peace. I went from feeling abandoned to feeling loved and wanted. Since I felt cared for and loved, feel-good chemicals were released that allowed my reasoning center to remain open, and I was able to understand what Jesus was sharing with me. It was while I was in that place of peace that He showed me what I had believed from that event for many years afterward; that I had to be independent and take care of myself, in case others left me all alone.

For years, I had been working hard and making sure I had a reserve of money, thinking it was because God made me independent and that I was a smart saver. In reality, I had a faulty belief that motivated me to react from a fear of being abandoned. Today, that memory no longer holds fear; it is rooted in the love of Jesus. I no longer focus on shivering in the cold bathwater feeling helpless and alone in the world. Jesus changed all of that. Instead, I laugh as I remember Jesus being with me, performing a *miracle* and instantly filling the tub up with warm water—and bubbles. That is the beauty of this healing model: Jesus, with whom we have a heart connection, is *with* us; we are connected, safe, and loved. When we feel safe and loved, we can emotionally and cognitively give and receive; we can give Him our pain and receive His healing love.

We have talked about fear and the effects it has on our well-being, but fear will not have the last say in this chapter—love will. Not just anyone's love, our Heavenly Father's love, a love that He gives because He is love. His unconditional love is a pure love that fulfills the deepest longing in our hearts—to be loved and accepted just as we are. When we experience God's love, it is not mere head knowledge; it is a heart experience. There is a place in His heart of love where He wants us to be deeply rooted so we can live in the fullness of His love, a place free from fear. In Ephesians 3:18, 19 Paul writes:

> *And I pray that you, being rooted and established in love, may*
> *have power, together with all the Lord's holy people, to grasp*
> *how wide and long and high and deep is the love of Christ,*
> *and to know this love that surpasses knowledge—that you may*
> *be filled to the measure of all the fullness of God.*

When I think of a root, a deep root attached to a plant, I think of how that root keeps the plant in place. Not only does it establish its position, it provides nutrients to help it thrive and grow. God created us to have a heart connection where we can experience His love to the fullest by being deeply rooted in His heart and nourished by His great love. The more we experience His love within us, we are more able to love ourselves and others as He intended.

The more we encounter His perfect love, the less room we have to fear.

It is true. His love changes everything.

An Immersion of Love

Jesus had healed and reframed so many of my traumatic memories taking toxic emotions and replacing them with His love and peace. He had uncovered faulty beliefs and replaced them with His truth, but I knew areas in my soul and body were still untouched by the love that casts out fear. I had encountered a touch of my Heavenly Father's love when He healed my neck, and I was continuing to experience the love of Jesus each time I met with Him in the quietness of my heart. Yet, I longed for more. I longed for His pure love to permeate every part of my being—spirit, soul, and body—down to a cellular level. I was recovering from severe adrenal fatigue caused by long-term Post-Traumatic Stress Disorder. In addition, my mom was contending for her life from a fast-growing glioblastoma brain tumor. My heart, my soul, and my body all needed a deep immersion of love and peace. In my heart, I knew I needed to be immersed in the deep ocean of His love, not just standing off the shore, knee-deep.

The mission trip to Brazil with Randy Clark, International Speaker and Founder of Global Awakening, and the Global Awakening Team had previously been planned. Mom still wanted me to go, so with my family's blessing, I went. Jesus moved in powerful ways. Hearts were set free, deaf ears opened, diseases lifted, and people were ministered to in powerful ways by the love and power of the Holy Spirit. The last night I stood off to the side as Randy spoke to the audience. I had given my all, spiritually, emotionally, and

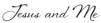

physically. I longed for the deep place of God's heart that David referenced in Psalm 42:1, 7.

> *As the deer pants for streams of water, so my soul pants for you, my God...deep calls to deep.*

I prayed, as I had done countless times in the weeks leading up to the trip, for God to immerse me in His love. Within a few moments of praying, dear friends of mine who were with me, along with two team members to whom I had ministered during the trip, walked over and began praying over me. I had prayed for so many others to experience the deep love of God; now, the very words that had come from my heart were flowing out of their mouths. As they prayed, His peace overwhelmed me, and I felt something pouring into me. My feet started filling up as if they were empty containers; then my legs. The liquid kept filling me until I could no longer stand. Lying on the floor, I let His love submerge me, immerse me. It permeated every cell and every part of my being. It is the purest love I have ever experienced. Closing my eyes, I saw water all around me and a bright light pierced through the water into me. I was lying at the bottom of an ocean. I was in the deep of His love!

As I lay on the cement floor of the church, His love saturated and coursed through me. It did not matter to me what anyone thought. All I felt and all I cared about was His unconditional, all-accepting, love—for me. I am not sure I will ever have the words to accurately explain the feeling of pure love I felt during that time. I remember thinking, "Everyone in the world has to experience this pure love of God!" As I lay there, I wished I had a gazillion billion containers of that ocean of love so I could give everyone in the world a drink so they could experience His true, unconditional, no-strings-attached, pure love. That is the love we are designed and wired to experience. That is the love that fills the deepest places of our hearts and souls. That is the love that changes us from the inside out. There is no other love like His, and I want you to drink of it, too.

Exercise: Deep Calls to Deep

Time: 10-20 Minutes

Physical Place: A quiet place away from distractions

Materials: Journal or paper and pen or pencil

Is your deep calling to Him with a longing to be immersed in your Heavenly Father's pure love? His love is for you, too. You do not have to get yourself cleaned up first, just ask. You do not have to do anything to earn it, just be open to receiving it. He longs to have a heart-to-heart relationship with you. He longs to pour His deep, pure love into the deepest parts of your heart and soul.

His love is the love that casts out fear. His love is gentle and kind. His love is patient and always available to you. His love is not manipulative or cunning. His love is not selfish or self-serving. He does not wonder what you have to give Him in return. He loves because He is love and you are worth loving.

For this exercise, you will meet Jesus in your Secret Place again and ask Him to take you to the deep where you can experience the love of your Heavenly Father. Start with your opening prayer of surrender and cleansing.

OPENING PRAYER

Jesus, thank you for creating me and wiring me for peace and love; I surrender my spirit, soul, and body to the Holy Spirit. I ask you to cleanse my physical and spiritual senses and attune them to you through the Holy Spirit.

Cleanse and purify my mind and imagination from all things that are not of you. Help me see and perceive clearly and help me dwell on that which is good and deserves praise—that which is true, noble, right, pure, lovely, and honorable. Help me dwell on you, your love for me, and your truth.

I surrender myself to you. Thank you for your Presence of Peace. I ask that you surround me with it now, and quiet all distractions. Guard my mind and heart as I go to the Secret Place to meet with you. Thank you, Jesus, for your goodness and your love for me.

When you are comfortable in your Secret Place and feel peace, invite Jesus to join you.

Jesus, please join me in our Secret Place.

When Jesus arrives, enjoy His Presence and the love and peace He brings, then journal what you are experiencing. Notice what Jesus is doing and listen for Him to tell you something.

What does Jesus do?

What does Jesus say?

What are you feeling emotionally and physically?

Since the time I was immersed in the deep of God's love, I have found it is easier for people to experience God's love by picturing one's self floating in a body of water. When people explain what they see in their mind or spirit, many mention a waterfall. Guess what you get to do now. Yes, practice floating in His love. When you are ready, ask Jesus to take you to the waterfall by a pool of water. It does not matter if you have been to an actual place like that before; use your imagination and spiritual eyes and go with Jesus to the one He wants you to visit.

Describe or draw the pool of water and waterfall...

When you are ready, ask Jesus to get into the water and float with you.

Jesus, will you please get into the water and float with me?

Take a few moments and float with Jesus absorbing the peace that is all around you. Then let your Heavenly Father know you long to experience His deep love.

Heavenly Father: I long to experience the depths of your love down to my cellular level. Please immerse me, saturate me, and fill my spirit, my soul, and my body with your pure, Holy love.

Thank you for your love, and for loving me without conditions. Thank you for loving me just as I am.

Give yourself time to experience His love and let His peace settle within you. Float in it; soak in it. Let His love seep in, little by little.

Take some time to journal afterward. Did you notice anything in your body or mind, such as more peace? Was there a release of some sort, such as tears? Did you experience His love in a new way or in a deeper measure? Did your soul experience emotions such as love, peace, happiness, calmness, inspiration, hope, or another positive emotion?

Do not be discouraged if you find this exercise difficult at first. As you continue to connect with Jesus, and as your heart heals, you will be able to receive more of His love and the love of your Heavenly Father. It is not a one-time prayer. Keep asking. Keep soaking. Keep receiving. Keep growing as you become firmly planted, firmly rooted, and firmly established in His love for you.

You are worth it, lovely one. You are worth it.

Before we walk through the healing of traumatic memories with Jesus, we need to have a heart-to-heart talk about something that can either keep

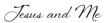

you from receiving the healing you need or walk you miles down the road in your healing journey with Jesus—forgiveness.

Forgiveness of others, yourself, and Father God.

CHAPTER TWENTY-FIVE

Joy in Freedom

Before my healing journey, it was hard for me to imagine a bright future. Stuck in the mire of past experiences and regrets, I felt like I took one step forward, then two steps back. I sought help periodically through the years for the symptoms, but it was not until my love encounter with God and Jesus walking me through my healing journey, that I found healing and freedom that lasted. Step-by-step, memory-by-memory; it was not a quick fix. We were dealing with many years, many hurts, many heart wounds, and thick walls of self-protection.

Walls of self-protection—they are sometimes necessary, especially when we are young. It is our only way of surviving at the time. Those walls of self-protection are not meant to stay up forever, and we often need help returning to the original event so that healing can take place. Why? *We* are trapped inside those thick walls. We cannot be who God created us to be and walk in our purpose when we are locked away in a fortress-turned-prison.

Jesus came to *restore* our hearts and *release* our destinies. We need Him to help take the walls down and lead us into bright open spaces where we can breathe clean air and soak up the sun. He knows why we built the walls, and He knows what is still behind them. He knows and cares because those walls enclose our hearts—hearts that were created to connect with God and receive His love; hearts that now carry deep wounds of hurt, trauma, and neglect caused by the actions of others, by sin, and by choices we have made ourselves.

When we build walls around our hearts and internalize the unprocessed trauma, we internalize the pain—along with those who caused the suffering. We harbor our offenders and lock them up with us in the rooms of our wounded, damaged hearts. We barricade them in, seal the door, and hope they will wither away along with the hurt they caused. We hang a "Do Not Access" sign on the door and resolve to steer clear of it, knowing that if we crack it even a fraction, they, along with the pain, will try to force their way out. Instead of withering away over time, however, we find they are very much alive in our hearts and thoughts. We have kept them alive with our resentment, hurt, anger, and bitterness. The pain, trauma, and the emotions that go along with it have not left at all. They are still there rancid and leaking toxins into our hearts, minds, and bodies—toxins that are byproducts of the wrong done and of unforgiveness.

The Power of Forgiveness

One thing became clear on my healing journey: I had to forgive those who caused my suffering. My offenders, along with the pain and toxic emotions, were taking up valuable space in my heart, space meant for God's peace, love, and joy. They were not only taking up space, but they also weighed me down, and I was emotionally tired of carrying them around. To fully forgive meant I had to open the door of my heart where I allowed those who had hurt me to reside, along with the pain. Thankfully, Jesus was there to help me. He knew that for me to be free from the past, I had to be free from those who wronged me. He also knew that the enemy feeds off of unforgiveness.

Unforgiveness is emotional tar that keeps us stuck in past hurts.

Unforgiveness gave the enemy access to walk right into my heart and wreak further havoc with my emotions and my thinking. It is a Biblical principle—one God knew was vital for our peace of mind and well-being. Jesus made a big deal about this principle when Peter asked him about forgiving others. Matthew 18:21-36 tells the Parable of the Servant who owed his master more than he could repay in his lifetime. Since he could not pay back the debt, the master ordered the servant, along with his wife and children, to be sold to repay it. The servant begged for mercy and asked for time to repay. The master, even knowing the servant could never repay it all, had pity on him and canceled the entire debt. His family was saved from being sold, and he was debt-free—all because his master, the one who had every right to demand payment, had mercy and forgave the entire debt owed.

How did the servant respond? Did he fall on his knees in thankfulness before his master, thanking him for such a gift that he did not deserve? Did he go home and tell his wife and kids how wonderful and merciful the master had been toward him? Did he share the grace that had been bestowed on him and forgive the debts of those who owed him? No. He went out and found a man who owed him a hundred silver coins—much less than what he had owed. He grabbed him and choked him, ordering him to repay the debt. The man begged for mercy and more time to repay it, but the servant refused to have pity or compassion on him; instead, he chose to hold resentment and unforgiveness in his heart and ordered the man thrown in prison until he could repay the debt owed. When fellow servants saw the mercy the master had shown the servant and how the servant refused to show mercy to the other man, they became angry and told the master. Very upset that the servant had not forgiven as he had been forgiven, the master had the servant brought before him and asked, "Shouldn't you have had mercy on your fellow servant just as I had on you?" He then handed the servant over to the jailors; the servant became a prisoner and was tortured.

The servant experienced total forgiveness of his debt, one he could never repay, yet he chose to hold resentment in his heart and demand payment of something owed him. He wanted the person who had wronged him to pay! His unwillingness to forgive cost him his freedom, took him away from his family, and caused him torment. He became a prisoner of his own resentment and unforgiveness.

Friend, when we do not forgive, it cost us freedom, too. We lock ourselves in the prison of our hearts with those who caused us pain. When we do not forgive and hold onto the debt the other person owes us from the wrong they have committed, the enemy moves in with that debt and brings torment to our lives. Instead of peace, we experience anger, bitterness, resentment, hate, and other negative emotions. We let it brew, leaking out toxins that affect us spiritually, emotionally, mentally, and physically.

Jesus understood the importance of forgiveness and modeled it for us in His dying breath (Luke 23:34). He understood that toxic emotions and unforgiveness go hand-in-hand negatively affecting every part of our being. Science is finding proof of its own. British researchers Peter Woodruff and Tom Farrow say emotions and forgiveness are intertwined finding that areas in the brain associated with forgiveness are deep in the *emotional centers* of the brain, not in the cortex usually associated with reasoned judgments.[26]

Medical professionals, pastors, and professional therapists see the need for forgiveness and the positive difference it makes in one's life. Below is a sampling of what others say about the power of forgiveness as it relates to the healing of unresolved trauma and health.

> *Chronic unforgiveness causes stress. Every time people think of their transgressor, their body responds. Decreasing your unforgiveness cuts down on your health risk. Now, if you can forgive, that can actually strengthen your immune system. (Everett Worthington, Ph.D.)*

> *In nurturing a patient's will to live, the first step is locating and treating past traumas. These poorly healed scars drain a significant portion of energy, and they hamper the body's capacity for self-defense. (David Servan-Schreiber, M.D., from AntiCancer)*

> *Forgiveness of self and others has been the most powerful predictor of both depression and suicide ideation. (Journal of Applied Sciences 2009, Vol.v9, Issue 19, pgs. 3598-3601)*

> *Forgiveness therapy is recognized as a powerful method of breaking cycles of hostility, anger and hatred. (Elliot 2010)*

> *Accomplishing emotional forgiveness transforms the person from a victim who is still controlled by the offender into an independent participant in life. (Elliot 2011)[27]*

I am not going to sugarcoat it. Walking through past memories and forgiving may be the hardest thing you will ever do. It was for me. It is also one of the most freeing and necessary things you will need to do to move forward. It takes courage. For those of us who have walked the path before you, we say, "In the end, it is worth it! You being free and whole is so gloriously worth it!"

God created us and understands that unforgiveness keeps us from moving forward. He does not want us to stay stuck in our past traumas, hurts, and offenses, nor does He want us taking on the burden of justice or revenge. We are to forgive and hand justice over to Him.

When we truly forgive, we release and relinquish. We release our offenders to Him and relinquish our right to revenge.

Romans 12:19 (TPT) says, Beloved, don't be obsessed with taking revenge, but leave that to God's righteous justice. For the Scriptures say: "If you don't take justice in your own hands, I will release justice for you," says the Lord.

Forgiving people is not justifying what they did; they still did wrong, and when wrong is done to us, something is taken from us. It could be our innocence, our peace of mind, our safety, or something or someone who meant a lot to us. Regardless of the type of offense, a debt is owed — one that requires restitution. When we forgive others, we are not sweeping the wrong and hurt under the rug. Far from it, we are bringing it to the open, handing our offenders and the wrong done to the Judge who is just, and freeing ourselves from the offense so we can be healed.

God is a God of love, and He is a God of justice. He takes the payment of debt seriously, so seriously, that He sent His son, Jesus, to become sin for humanity's wrongdoings. Jesus took the punishment for every wrong and sinful thing we would do as well as every wrong and sinful act that would be committed against us. Because Jesus took the punishment for all humanity, He has the right to release justice. As we forgive and relinquish our rights to dole out justice, we release our offenders to Jesus for Him to work in their lives as well as our own.

I remember the time Jesus whispered to me that He had died for my offenders, too. I did not know what to do with that statement. I went from being angry at Him to thanking Him. If He had forgiven and died for the worst of the worst offenders, then He had the right to bring justice. He also had the right to bring healing to their hearts if they opened them up to Him.

Over time, I realized that hurt people hurt people. When walking through forgiveness, it helped when I asked Jesus to give me compassion for the people who had hurt me; sometimes I knew their background and why they acted out and hurt others; other times I did not. Having compassion did not diminish their wrong or the justice that still needed to be served, but it allowed me to see them as people, instead of just by their actions.

Forgiveness is needed and required to be truly free—free to be filled with God's healing love, peace, and joy.

When you forgive trespasses against you and allow Jesus to cleanse your heart where the trespassers and the pain once were, you will have bright, clean spaces that can be filled with His love, peace, and joy. You are too valuable to have anyone besides Jesus and His love in your heart.

To show you a picture of how unforgiveness can take up space in our hearts and keep us from experiencing healing and God's peace, let us go on a visual journey. Picture yourself working in your yard. It is summer, and your neighbor digs up a plant you have been admiring in her flower garden. She gives it to you as a gift, and you have the perfect place for it! It will look great on your sun porch. Walking into your garage, you scan the shelves searching for the ideal container. Your eyes land on a colorful, unique can that has been sitting in the same place since you moved in, at least ten years. You are creative and decide it is finally time to put that can to use for something better than just sitting on a shelf. Taking the can down, you pry the lid off. Whew! A rancid stench meets your nose from the black goopy liquid that now looks like muck. You cannot put the plant in the muck; the muck will kill the plant. No, you need a container that is empty of muck, so you do the hard work; only a completely clean can and the best potting soil will do for this! You empty out the muck, clean the inside of the can, and then fill the container with rich potting soil. With a sense of satisfaction, you place your new plant into the soil and give it some love as you give it a fresh drink of water. Stepping back with a smile, you admire your potted plant in its colorful container that is now sitting on a table on your sun porch. Yep, it was worth the extra work. You have created a masterpiece.

You, my friend, are worth the work. Jesus wants you to be the masterpiece He created you to be, inside and out. The Master wants to help clean out the muck, cleanse you, and plant you in the fertile soil of His love and peace. Just as Jesus walked this road before you, He can walk it with you now. He has overcome, so He can help you overcome. He has forgiven everything you have ever done, so He can give you the strength to forgive those who have wronged you. When Jesus takes us to a door in our heart and asks us to let someone out, He helps us as we address the person and the pain. He helps walk us through forgiving that person and releasing the toxic emotions that have built up with all the hurt and muck. Jesus walks the offender out so He can make our hearts whole. Jesus takes the pain, the sorrow, the bitterness, and the anger, cleanses the space, and plants something beautiful.

Jesus chose to stay connected in a heart relationship with His Heavenly Father up to His last breath. He chose to forgive those who knowingly and unknowingly wronged Him, those who walked away, who abandoned Him, who rejected Him, who abused Him, who spit on Him, who scorned Him, who made fun of Him, and those who beat and whipped Him unmercifully. Jesus chose to forgive them all. He chooses to forgive you just as He chooses to forgive me. Forgive for Jesus' sake. Forgive for your sake. Forgive for the sake of the ones you love. You deserve to be the masterpiece God designed you to be—in every area of your life.

Here are a few stories of others who have walked through healing journeys with Jesus. May they encourage you as you walk through yours in the area of forgiveness.

Relief from Grief and Back Pain

One day my friend Raul shared with me that he was experiencing pain in a specific part of his upper back. It had started that week for no apparent reason and had been coming and going for several years. I asked if I could pray for him, and what began as a simple prayer for the physical pain to leave turned into something else as Jesus showed us that some emotional tar of

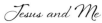

unforgiveness and grief were involved. Unforgiveness that my friend did not even realize was there until Jesus helped him see it.

Kimberly opened in prayer and invited me to picture a place in my mind where I feel safe and at peace. The beach is my favorite place to go, so I imagined myself there. We invited Jesus to join me on the beach. As Jesus and I stood looking out over the water, we asked Him if there was anything He wanted to reveal to me about the pain. A picture of my mom came to mind and sadness overwhelmed me. I realized it was the month of December; the same month my mom had passed away seven years earlier. Jesus brought back to mind how that Christmas Eve when she passed away that I had shoved down all feelings of sadness because it was supposed to be a happy time and I didn't want to be a downer to those around me.

Kimberly explained how our feelings can go down to the cellular level, and we asked Jesus if sadness or grief was showing up as pain in my back. As we asked Jesus this, I saw the painful place in my upper back take the shape of a heart, and I felt it begin to pulsate like a heartbeat. I told Jesus I missed my mom, and I placed my sadness and grief in a box and handed it to Him.

When Kimberly asked me what Jesus was doing with the box, I told her, "He's just holding onto it." Kimberly mentioned that when Jesus holds onto something, it may be because we are still holding onto something, too, and He wants to say or do more. We asked Jesus to reveal if I was holding onto anything or if I needed to forgive anyone; Jesus revealed to me that I needed to forgive my mom. She hadn't accepted my wife and how God created her, which had deeply hurt me. I forgave my mom for not seeing my beautiful wife as Jesus created and saw her.

After I forgave my mom, Jesus threw the box of sadness and grief into the ocean. We then asked Him to take the pain away and replace the sadness and grief with Himself and His peace. With a big smile, Jesus stood in front of me on the beach and reached through me! His hand went through my heart and touched the painful place in my upper back.

The pinpointed pain diminished until it was gone entirely. That day, Jesus healed my emotions, my heart, and my body! To this day, that place in my upper back is pain-free and the sadness I felt every Christmas has been replaced with peace.

Jesus is amazing! He knows everything about us and how experiences affect us down to a cellular level. Pain is the body's way of informing us something is wrong. I am not saying that all pain occurs because of unforgiveness; I do not have all the answers. What I do know is that when we invite Jesus into the picture, He knows what we need in that moment. He is the safe person we can connect with, and He knows where we should go to gain the freedom that is rightfully ours. The freedom that He can bring us into when we are willing to go with Him—regardless of what has happened in the past.

Lifting the Weight of Responsibility

This story belongs to Joan. She is a survivor of war, abuse, and the weight of responsibility. This is just a snippet of the beautiful healing Jesus is doing in her heart, soul, and body after years of trauma. When Joan was young, her country was at war with a neighboring country. It became the norm for her to run for cover when the bullets and missiles started flying. It was one of those memories that Jesus took her back to so He could lift off the weight that had been put on her eight-year-old shoulders one day, a burden that she had been carrying for thirty-three years.

As Kimberly led me through my healing journey that day, Jesus met me in a boat. I felt so much joy because He was with me. As we sat in the boat together, He told me, "I know all the details of your childhood Joan, and I'm here to heal them." He put His arm around me and continued, "I hold you together...all the pieces, all the fragments...and I'm fusing them together so you can be a whole person again." As He said those words, I felt a sense of safety and security that I'd never felt before. Peace began to settle into my body.

Jesus first took me to a memory when I was eight years old. We had just run for cover from the missiles, and my mom fearfully showed me where all of our passports were; she wanted me to have them should my parents be killed in the fighting. Showing them to me, she told me I was responsible for my sisters who were younger than I. I felt a great weight of responsibility come on my small eight-year-old shoulders, along with the fear that my parents were going to be killed.

As I saw the scene play out again in my mind, I saw Jesus sitting with me, holding my hand as my mom placed the weight of that on my shoulders. Jesus showed me that it was at that moment that I believed the lie that I was responsible for the safety of my siblings, which led to years of my worrying about them and trying to control and fix things for them to keep them at peace. I also carried the fear that if something did happen to any of them, I would be at fault and blamed, as I had failed to protect them.

The next memory Jesus brought up was when I was eleven. During a civil war, my parents sent my sisters and me to a different part of the country to live with relatives so we would be out of the direct line of fire while they stayed behind. Unfortunately, that was the same family as a relative who had been sexually abusing me already for several years. For months, we had zero contact with my mom or dad, and I feared both had been killed. For months, I thought I was an orphan, an orphan responsible for her sisters, an orphan who couldn't escape her abuser.

Returning from school one afternoon, I found my mom standing in the family room of my aunt's house. I dropped my book bag and flew into her arms. She was alive! She hugged me so tight that I didn't want to let go; that hug was one of the rare times I remember feeling like my mom truly cared for me. She stayed for a few days and then left us—again. My mom, who was supposed to protect me, left me for another three months in that situation until my parents thought it safe enough for us to return home.

When we walked through forgiveness, Jesus asked me to forgive my mom. It was hard but freeing. I let her out of my heart and brought her to Jesus.

I forgave her for putting the weight of having to take care of my sisters on me. I forgave her for how it still affected me into adulthood. I forgave her for sending me away from her and into a situation where I was abused.

As I forgave her, I realized that what had happened to me had become part of my identity, an identity that was not whom God created me to be. When I was done forgiving my mom, I asked Jesus to bless her. He put His hand on my mom's shoulder and commended her for being strong and doing what she thought was right at the time. I realized that my mom had been reacting out of fear as she wasn't sure she and my dad would be alive to take care of us.

When Kimberly asked Jesus to lift off the coat of responsibility my mom had placed around my shoulders, He lifted it off my eight-year-old shoulders and began smashing it in pieces under His feet. Destroyed, it could not go on me again. In its place, He gave me paddings similar to what football players wear. Positioning them on my shoulders, Jesus said, "These are for strengthening and conditioning to break through things."

I knew then that breakthrough was indeed happening. When we asked Jesus to give me a new memory, I saw my mom with Jesus. I walked up with my football pads on, and the three of us hugged, a group hug, a tight one, just like the one my mom gave me after not seeing me all those months. In that moment, I felt a piece of me being restored.

Joan's journey of healing continues, with a gift from Jesus to help her with further breakthroughs into the painful places where trauma has settled. Joan later shared that since Jesus lifted the weight of responsibility, she no longer feels the urge to worry about her sisters, nor does she feel responsible that if something happens to them, she is to blame. She has also let go of the fear that something may happen to her young sons; she knows now that she shares the responsibility of raising them with her husband and Jesus. They are all in God's hands.

I do not know what you have been through in life, but Jesus does. He can walk you through it all and give you the courage to forgive those who have

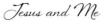

hurt you. The next exercise will help you do that. You can do this, friend. Jesus will be with you, each step of the way.

Exercise: Freedom in Forgiveness

Time: 15-20 Minutes

Physical Place: A quiet place away from distractions

Materials: Journal or paper and pen or pencil

Are you ready to see if anyone is taking up valuable space in your heart? Some people may instantly come to mind, but for this exercise, you will ask Jesus whom He specifically wants to highlight. It is amazing how many people I needed to forgive on my healing journey. It is a continual process in life, and I have included additional copies of this exercise in the Healing Journal Workbook. I have made it a habit of doing a weekly, sometimes daily, check. I want my heart as full of His love, peace, and joy as possible.

This exercise can take 15 to 20 minutes. Sometimes longer, sometimes shorter, depending on the depth of the hurt and the number of offenses you need to forgive. This exercise is one of the most critical steps in your healing journey, and it will take you miles down the road in a short amount of time. Please do not skip it.

Each piece of this exercise is important, and you will be led through it step-by-step. With Jesus beside you, you will see and release from your heart those who hurt you. You will have a voice as you forgive and tell them what they did was wrong and how it affected you. You will learn how to ask Jesus to uncover lies you believed when you were wounded and how to break agreement with those lies. You will learn how to use your authority in Jesus Christ to evict any unholy spirits that camped out and fed off the unforgiveness. At the end of the exercise, you will finish by asking Jesus to heal and restore any affected areas of your spirit, soul, and body.

As you walk through this exercise, it is okay for emotions of anger, hurt, resentment, bitterness, or other negative emotions to surface. Do not ignore them or try to suppress them. Let them rise and give them to Jesus. Let Him cleanse your heart and emotions and fill those areas with His love and peace.

For this exercise, I like to picture Jesus with me where I am physically. For instance, I have a chair in my study where I read my Bible and have devotions. I picture Jesus sitting in a chair next to me, helping me through this exercise.

This prayer will get you started.

OPENING PRAYER

Jesus: Thank you that you care about me and what has happened to me. Thank you for forgiving me of all my wrongdoings.

I surrender my spirit, soul, and body to the Holy Spirit and ask you to release your Peace within me and around me. Guard my heart and mind as I work through forgiving others with you, Jesus. Quiet all distractions and bind up any unholy spirits that may try to interfere with our time and this exercise. Thank you, Jesus, for your blood that you shed for me and for the forgiveness of sins. Please give me the courage to forgive from my heart those who have wronged me.

When you feel at peace and know Jesus is with you, imagine your heart in your hands. Some doors on the outside of your heart lead to places inside of it. Several of them may even have a sign on the outside of the door that says "Do Not Access."

Show your heart to Jesus and ask Him which door to open first; then ask Him to help you open the door and go in with you. If things seem dreary or dark inside an area in your heart, it is okay. Ask Jesus to shine His light so you can see clearly.

Jesus, will you show me which door to open and the person I need to forgive right now? Please help me open that door and go inside with me.

Who is behind the door?

What is he or she doing?

The prayer below will walk you through addressing the offender, forgiving, and releasing him or her to Jesus as well as relinquishing your right to make the person pay. You will have a voice as you address (1) what the offender did to you, (2) how it affected you and your life, and (3) how it made you feel.

(Name of the offender) _____ what you did to me was wrong. When you (list the wrongs done to you)...

_____

it (state how it affected you and your life)...

_____

Your actions/words made me feel...

_____

I'm choosing now, with Jesus' help, to forgive you as Jesus forgave me. I forgive you for the wrong you did to me, how you made me feel, and the effects it had on my spirit, soul, and body.

Jesus, I ask you to forgive (name of offender) _____ for (his / her) offenses against me, for how (his / her) actions made me feel, and how the actions/words affected me.

Help open the heart of _____ so you can heal (his / her) heart also. Bless _____ and work in (his / her) life in a redemptive way.

Jesus, I release _____ to you, and I relinquish my right to make (him / her) pay by getting revenge or bringing punishment upon (him / her). Jesus, I'm putting _____ in your hands now. Please walk _____ out of my heart.

Walk the person over to Jesus. Jesus will walk the person out of your heart. When Jesus returns (He always has a big smile on His face when He comes back to me.), give Jesus permission to clean out and cleanse that area of your heart where your offender once resided along with any unholy effects and toxic emotions.

Jesus, my heart is yours. Forgive me for the bad thoughts and toxic emotions I harbored in my heart and mind against my offender. Please cleanse that space in my heart and mind now.

Clean out all toxic emotions (anger, hurt, bitterness, revenge, et cetera). If I've put up any walls in this space, please remove them so this space is open and free to be filled with your love. Jesus, I ask that you cleanse and purify me from all the unholy effects (name of offender's) _____ transgressions against me have had on my spirit, my soul, and my body.

What do you see Jesus doing?

What are you feeling?

When Jesus is done cleansing that area,
ask Him to fill it with His love and peace.

Jesus, please fill that clean space in my heart now with your love and peace.

Take some time to journal what you are seeing Jesus do in your heart and what you are experiencing during this time. Do you feel different such as lighter, cleaner, relieved?

You are doing great; just a few more steps to go. We can have faulty belief systems from believing a lie in the midst of the hurt. Ask Jesus if you believe any lies from the experience. If so, write the lies in the section below.

Jesus, please bring to my attention any lies I believe from the past experience. Do I believe any lies about...

Myself?

You (Jesus) or Father God?

The person who hurt me?

If Jesus showed you anything, tell Him you are sorry for agreeing (knowingly or unknowingly) with the lie, renounce the lie, and break agreement with it.

Jesus: Thank you for revealing the lie(s) to me. I'm sorry for taking agreement with the lie(s) that _____.

I ask you to forgive me, and I receive your forgiveness. I now renounce and break all agreements that I knowingly or unknowingly made with the lie(s).

Now ask Jesus to reveal His truth and plant it deep in your heart and mind.

Jesus, what is your truth?

What does Jesus say?

———◆—◆—◆◆—◆—◆———

Jesus, I ask you to plant the truth that (state out loud the truth Jesus shared with you) deep in my heart and mind.

Journal anything you are seeing or experiencing...

Great job! As the enemy likes to camp out on unforgiveness and lies, now is the perfect time to remind him you have forgiven your offender and broken agreement with the lie. That space is now empty of offense and has been cleaned and filled with Jesus' love. No longer does the room have any space for him. Here is a prayer I like to use to give any unholy spirits that were attached to the offense and unforgiveness a swift kick out on their ugly backsides. Use the authority you have in Jesus and pray it aloud. Let the devil know his rights are canceled and that he has to pack his bags and leave.

In the name of Jesus Christ, I command any unholy spirits that once had a right to this offense to cease all torment and harm. I've forgiven (name of person you forgave and released to Jesus) _____ and (his / her) wrongs against me.

(Name of person you forgave) _____ no longer lives in my heart. Jesus has cleansed that area in my heart and filled it with His love.

I repent and renounce any past thought or behavior that allowed unholy spirits to attach to me in any way. You no longer have any right to stay, and you must pack your bags and leave now without throwing any tantrums or causing any damage. Go now where Jesus sends you. I now place the cross and blood of Jesus Christ between myself and the unholy spirits that left. You are not welcome back!

Journal anything you experienced during this prayer...

When saying the above prayer, people have shared different experiences with me. Some took a deep breath and felt a release when they exhaled. Others have felt, or seen with their spiritual eyes, something gray or dark leave from their stomach or the top of their heads. Others have noticed that the message they continually heard in their minds surrounding the experience has stopped. Others have experienced an indescribable peace and lightness. Some people haven't felt anything different. I once prayed the prayer above and didn't feel anything, so I asked Jesus to give me a picture if something was there and had to leave. He gave me a picture of a small creature throwing clothes into a suitcase. He slammed it shut and sulked out the door of my heart. I smiled, then I giggled, then I broke out laughing. Jesus had just healed and redeemed another part of my heart, another part of my life.

You did excellent heart work! End the exercise by asking Jesus to heal any place, physically, spiritually, emotionally, and mentally, that has been suffering from the offense.

Jesus, I need your healing touch. Please heal me physically, spiritually, emotionally, and mentally from all suffering I've been experiencing from the offense of the person I forgave and released to you.

Pay attention to your body and emotions.
Write out what you are experiencing...

Some people notice instant physical healing, like my friend Raul; for others, it is the foundation of the healing that happens in increments as other parts of their heart and soul heal. Others notice a lifting of depression. Others experience joy and peace. Again, your experience will be unique because you and your journey are unique. Regardless of if you feel anything different in your body at the moment, remember you are an integrated being—spirit, soul, and body. When one is affected, the other two are affected in some measure as well.

Finish your time with Jesus by thanking Him.

Jesus, I thank you, and I receive your healing. Thank you for walking with me and for your redeeming grace.

Congratulations, you made it all the way through your first forgiveness exercise with Jesus! Whether you realize it now or not, you just participated in some major heart surgery. Do not be surprised if you are emotionally and physically tired; it is normal, and taking time to recover is important. I encourage you to spend a few days meeting Jesus in your Secret Place. Take extra time to rest in His peace and thank Him for your healing thus far. Soak in His Presence. He will let you know when it is time to move on to the next chapter and exercise.

Well done, my friend. Well done.

CHAPTER TWENTY-SIX

Heavy Garments

Just as it is essential to talk about forgiving others and the positive effects forgiveness has on our spiritual, mental, emotional, and physical health, it is equally important to address the fact that at times, we need to forgive ourselves.

Have you ever wondered why it is easier to forgive others than yourself? Remember the devil is a bully. Shame is his last, big-ditch effort to keep us out of our Heavenly Father's arms. He tried it with Jesus; he tries it on us. He wants to shame us for things we have done as well as feel the shame others heap upon us through their words or actions against us. Regardless of the circumstances, satan's goal is to isolate us, then make us think everyone has abandoned us.

Jesus felt abandoned and forsaken too. Imagine only knowing love, no sin, then to *be* full sin. On the cross, Jesus cried out, "My God, My God, why have you forsaken me?" Add to that, most of His disciples abandoned Him (Matthew 27:46). One wonders what shame and humiliation Jesus felt as He hung on the cross naked, exposed, jeered at, mocked, and ridiculed. People spit upon him and hurled words of shame and insults. The demonic world came to take their best shot as well; they all wanted a piece of the prize. After all, they were finally killing their greatest nemesis.

Oh for the joy set before Him (We were the joy!), He stayed the course. He scorned the shame and paid our price. I love the order of the wording in Hebrews 12:2 "For the joy set before him he endured the cross, scorning its shame, and sat down at the right hand of the throne of God."

Surprise, satan! Your dirty deeds just brought to pass God's plan of redemption. Even though satan could not stop Jesus from fulfilling His mission, it does not mean he put the tool of shame away; he uses it against God's people as often as possible.

Satan desperately wants us to play his blame game so we will stay caught in the cycle of blame, shame, and punishment and not focused on God's healing. He wants us to blame others for how we feel as well as ourselves.

> *Blaming others leads to feelings of anger, bitterness, and resentment toward your offenders; blaming yourself leads to feelings of guilt, shame, and self-condemnation.*

While Jesus came to lift off our garments of despair, the devil uses our hurts and woundings to whisper lies about our worth so we will run and hide from others—and from God. The devil knows that when we blame ourselves, we take on the garment of guilt and believe his lie that we do not deserve forgiveness; we feel that we are just not worthy.

After we put on the garment of guilt, satan throws over our shoulders the garment of shame as we believe the lie that what we have done is so bad it is unforgivable and that God is disappointed with us or angry at us, and would not want to forgive us, nor would anyone else. We withdraw into ourselves and start to stay away from others. We begin to believe that what we did is part of who we are.

After the shame, satan lays the heavily-weighted garment of self-condemnation around our shoulders as we believe the lie that the only way to make things right is if we are punished. If there is no one around to punish us, we find ways of punishing ourselves through negative behaviors that harm us or by denying ourselves the experience of healing and living in the fullness of life that God wants for us. We feel there is no freedom until we have been punished enough.

When we blame ourselves, our hearts and true selves are buried underneath garments of pain, guilt, shame, and self-condemnation; garments Jesus wants us to hand Him so that we can receive His healing and walk in freedom. Jesus' garments were stripped from Him at the cross as He took on our sin, the guilt and shame that comes with the sin, the condemnation, and our due punishment. God put it all on Jesus so it could all be crucified with Him. Our garments of old were stripped at the cross too so we could have the righteous robe of Jesus upon His death. As children of God, those old heavy garments do not belong to us anymore.

> *He became sin, so God made him who had no sin to be sin for us so that in him we might become the righteousness of God (2 Corinthians 5:21).*

> *I delight greatly in the Lord; my soul rejoices in my God. For he has clothed me with garments of salvation and arrayed me in a robe of his righteousness, as a bridegroom adorns his head like a priest, and as a bride adorns herself with her jewels (Isaiah 61:10).*

Jesus would never think of putting dirty garments on top of His robe of righteousness—a robe that is also yours and mine. When we willingly pick up or allow satan to hang robes of guilt, shame, and self-condemnation on top of our robe of righteousness, it is a dishonor to Jesus and what He did for us on the cross. It is time to put the devil in his place and tell Jesus we are sorry for wearing dirty robes over our robe of righteousness. It is time to trust Jesus' love and let Him lift off our garments of despair so we can see our robe of righteousness in all its splendor and walk in our true identity as His righteous bride.

Regardless of how devastating an experience was or how much guilt and shame one is carrying, Jesus is the One who can remove the garments that no longer belong to you or me. He did that for my friend, Miranda. I am grateful to my friend for being courageous and letting me share her story with you. She is an amazing woman of God who has experienced firsthand the healing grace that only Jesus can bring. I had the honor of leading her through this healing exercise thirty-three years after the devastating event. For three decades, she could not shake off the heavy garments of guilt, shame, and self-condemnation the enemy had tied tightly around her neck—until Jesus came into the picture and asked her to hand them to Him.

Miranda was in the process of moving to another state to start a new chapter in life. As she drove the truck with her 1½-year-old son in the back seat, she noticed several cars parked ahead along the edge of the road. A man, who had been standing on the side of traffic talking to a person in one of the cars, suddenly stepped back into her lane just as she drove by the row of cars. With no time to swerve, my friend hit him, throwing him several hundred feet. As my friend shared her story, I heard and felt the pain of that moment. She felt so alone, just her and her baby boy, in a devastating experience, caught miles between what she had left behind and her new life ahead. Jesus was about to change that.

Jesus took me back to the memory as I was coming up on the line of cars parked alongside the road. When I glanced in my rearview mirror, I saw Jesus sitting in the back seat of the truck with my son. A sense of peace came over me. Jesus stayed through the whole event. He was in the truck with me as the man stepped into my lane; after I came to a stop Jesus gently told me, "It wasn't your fault." For years I couldn't shake that it was my fault, that I could have slammed on the brakes faster or harder, that I should have done something differently. Even though "Not Guilty" had been the verdict at the trial as well, it wasn't until I heard Jesus tell me those words that I truly believed it in my spirit.

When I got out of the truck, I saw Jesus standing next to the man lying on the ground, talking to him. It brought me comfort to know he didn't die alone. I never had closure with the man as I wasn't allowed to go near him, but Jesus was there now, and we asked Jesus if I could come over and tell the man I was sorry. Through sobs and with Jesus by my side, I told the man I was sorry for causing his death and for leaving his family without a son and a fiancé without a life with him. Jesus turned to me and asked me to give Him the guilt I had been carrying all those years. Little by little,

I began putting the years of guilt into His hands. Jesus put it all in a bag and slung it over His shoulder, saying "This isn't yours to carry anymore."

As we continued to move through forgiveness and giving Jesus all the shame and guilt that had built up in my heart throughout the years tied to the accident, Jesus began wiping black stuff off my heart. When He stopped cleaning, if there was any black left, we knew more forgiveness needed to happen. Jesus asked me to forgive the man for stepping back into my lane. As I forgave the man, I realized I held anger and bitterness toward him for changing my world forever. I also realized I had taken on the anger and bitterness I believed his parents and fiancé felt against me. I let the anger and resentment go as I forgave them.

Turning to Jesus, I asked Him to forgive me. He did of course, and then He asked me to forgive myself! That was hard, but as I did, the last of the black left my heart, and an overwhelming peace flooded my heart and soul. My heart had gone from black to bright red. We asked Jesus to fill my cleansed heart with His Presence and love. He did, and He added the word 'JOY' in white capital letters across my now beautiful, bright-red, healed heart.

The memory of the accident was so traumatic that the memory was deeply ingrained in my mind. We asked Jesus to cleanse with His blood the neural pathways of the memory from all trauma, guilt, and shame and to remove all triggers set up within the memory at the time of the event. When Kimberly asked Jesus to cleanse the neural pathways, a sharp pain began in the back right side of my head. With the authority of Jesus, we commanded any unholy spirits attached to the accident to leave. They could no longer have a hold on me. The pain left as well as the sick feeling I had carried in my stomach for years!

With all the obstacles out of the way, Jesus began to cleanse and heal the neural pathways of that memory. I saw and felt Jesus blowing cleansing water into my head through a straw. It was a peaceful, gentle cleansing that washed the pain out of the memory and replaced it with His love and peace. Jesus is wonderful! No longer am I in a constant state of shame and guilt, for Jesus has moved me into the still calm waters of His love and redemptive grace.

Jesus, in His kind and gentle ways, continues to bring healing to my friend from other memories of that experience. For those who are wondering about her young son, Jesus showed Miranda that He was in the backseat protecting him; He was a shield for him from the impact and the flying glass. As we prayed for trauma to be removed from her son from the accident, Miranda watched as Jesus held her little boy in His arms and removed shattered glass from his clothing. Jesus finished reframing the memory by praying a Father's blessing over her son.

Jesus. Savior. Healer. Redeemer. He is One in whom we can trust to take us to the hard places and get us *through* them. When we understand that He is with us, even in the darkest of circumstances, He and His love change things.

Jesus' love changes us from the inside out.

I do not know what you have been through or what garments may be covering up your white robe of righteousness, but Jesus is *with* you, waiting for you to hand the garments to Him. Ask Him if you have some garments to give to Him during the next exercise.

You will feel so much lighter.

Exercise: Handing Over Garments of Guilt, Shame, and Self-Condemnation

Time: 15-20 Minutes
Physical Place: A quiet place away from distractions
Materials: Journal or paper and pen or pencil

Jesus longs for us to walk in freedom unbound by the guilt of our wrongs. In Him, we are blameless and righteous before our Father. Jesus wants us to bring everything we have done, with our feelings and thoughts to

Him to cleanse, redeem, and restore. When we bring it all to Him, we *release* it to Him and *relinquish* the right to punish ourselves. Romans 8:1 points out that "There is now no condemnation for those who are in Christ Jesus." It is time to give Jesus the garments that do not belong to us and return to focusing on the robe of righteousness Jesus gave each of us when we accepted Him as Savior. It is time to let ourselves out of the prison of our own hearts and run free with Him, so get on your running shoes. You are loved, worthy, and about to find out that you can run farther and faster without those heavy garments weighing you down.

Similar to the exercise in the last chapter on forgiving others, it is okay for emotions to surface. It is important to give all of them to Jesus. This exercise can take 15 to 20 minutes, sometimes longer, sometimes shorter, depending on the depth of the experience, and the amount of guilt and shame you may be carrying. The important thing to remember is that Jesus adores you. He is not disappointed or upset with you. He loves you, and when you walk through this *with* Him, you will know it is His perfect time for you to find sustainable healing in this area.

Similar to the last exercise, picture Jesus with you in your physical space. This prayer will get you started.

OPENING PRAYER

Jesus, I invite you to sit beside me now and walk me through this exercise. Thank you for always being here for me. Thank you that you care for me and love me despite my wrongdoings. Thank you for forgiving me and for taking all my punishment on the cross. I ask you to guard my mind and heart and bind up any unholy spirits that may try to interfere with our time together. Fill me now with your peace and give me the courage to forgive myself and hand you those garments that do not belong to me.

When you feel at peace with Jesus beside you, imagine your heart in your hands. You see the doors on the outside leading into your heart. Show your heart to Jesus and ask Him if there is a door that leads to a place where you yourself are locked up.

Jesus, will you please point out the door you want me to open? Will you help me open it and go with me into my heart now?

Once inside your heart, what do you see?

Are you there?

What age are you?

What are you doing?

What heavy garments are around your shoulders?

Ask Jesus to show you why you have locked yourself up. He may tell you or take you back to a memory.

Jesus, please let me know why I have locked myself up in my heart.

What does Jesus tell you and or show you?

Before forgiving yourself, ask Jesus if there is anyone who needs your forgiveness in regards to why you are wearing the garments of guilt, shame, or self-condemnation. He may ask you to talk to him or her later in person, but for this exercise in this moment, do it with Jesus in the quietness of your heart.

Jesus, is there anyone's forgiveness I need to ask for in relation to the experience where I put on the garments of guilt, shame, and self-condemnation?

If Jesus shows you anyone, you can use this prayer while picturing the person there with you and Jesus. It is also a good template to use should Jesus ask you to go in person to apologize and ask for forgiveness.

(Name of person you hurt) _____, I'm sorry for...(list actions or words against the person you hurt._____)

I'm sorry for the impact my actions and words had on your heart and life. What I did was wrong: please forgive me. I pray that Jesus will heal the wounds I've caused you.

If there is a response from the person you are forgiving, journal it here...

Ask Jesus to heal the person of your hurt and bless him or her.

Jesus, will you please take away the harmful effects my actions had on (the person you hurt) _____. Cleanse (his / her) spirit, soul, and body with your cleansing blood and heal (him / her). Fill those places where I wounded _____ with your love and peace. Thank you, Jesus, for caring about us all. I ask you to bless _____ now.

Now, ask Jesus to forgive you and hand over the heavy garments.

◆◆◆◆◆◆

Jesus, I'm sorry for the wrong I did that hurt _____ and I'm sorry for carrying all this guilt and shame. Will you please forgive me?

What does Jesus say or do?

Hand Jesus the garments of guilt, shame, self-condemnation, and all the negative emotions and thoughts that go with them. If you have a hard time doing so, ask Jesus to help you.

◆◆◆◆◆◆

Jesus, I don't want to carry the guilt, shame, or self-condemnation any longer. I release all these heavy garments and negative feelings and thoughts to you and relinquish all rights to punish myself in any way.

What does Jesus do with the garments, feelings, and thoughts?

What does Jesus say to you?

◆◆◆◆◆◆

Jesus, thank you for taking my guilt and shame and the condemnation I had toward myself. It no longer belongs to me. I ask you now to cleanse that area in my heart and all the areas in my life that were affected by it. Please fill those places now with your love, acceptance, and peace.

What do you see Jesus doing?

What are you experiencing?

Let the "you" in your heart know you are free, and ask Jesus to reunite the once locked-up you with who you are today.

(Your name) _____, you are free! As of (date _____), the garments of guilt, shame, and self-condemnation no longer belong to you. Jesus, now that I am no longer locked up in my heart, please reunite that part of me with who I am today.

Take a few minutes and journal what you are experiencing spiritually, emotionally, mentally, physically...

You are making great progress, continue and ask Jesus if you have any lies or faulty beliefs from that experience. If so, write the lies in the section below.

Jesus, please bring to my attention any lies or faulty beliefs I believe from the past experience. Am I believing a lie about...

Myself?

Father God?

Jesus?

Someone else?

If Jesus reveals something, it is important to tell Him you are sorry for making an agreement, knowingly or unknowingly, with the lie, renounce it, and break agreement with it. We want to get to the root, dig up the lie, and plant His truth so you will never want to put those heavy garments on again.

———

Jesus: Thank you for revealing the lie(s) and faulty belief(s) to me! I want your truth planted instead.

I ask you to forgive me for taking agreement with (name lie or faulty belief), and I receive your forgiveness. I now renounce and break all agreements I knowingly or unknowingly made with the lie(s) and faulty belief(s).

Jesus, what truth do you want to plant in my heart and mind now?

Write the truth that Jesus shares with you in the prayer below.

———

Jesus, thank you for planting your truth that (write truth)

Please plant the truth deep in my heart and in my mind. Water it with your love and with your living Word. Please help me run to you and My Heavenly Father when I get hurt. Thank you for your love for me.

Remember what is next from the exercise in the last chapter? Yep! Letting the enemy know he cannot camp out in your soul anymore. Use the authority you have in Jesus, and let any unholy spirits know they are no longer welcome and must go. Remember to say it aloud.

In the name of Jesus Christ, I command any unholy spirits that once had a right to this past event to cease all torment and harm. I've forgiven others and myself as Jesus has forgiven me. Jesus has cleansed the areas in my heart and filled it with His love.

I repent and renounce any past thought or behavior that allowed unholy spirits to attach in any way. You no longer have any right to stay, and you must pack your bags and leave now without throwing any tantrums or causing any damage. Go now where Jesus sends you. I now place the cross and blood of Jesus Christ between myself and the unholy spirits that left. You are not welcome back!

Journal anything you experienced during this prayer...

Ask Jesus to heal any place, physically, spiritually, emotionally, or mentally, that has been suffering from the event and the guilt, shame, and self-condemnation.

Jesus, I need your healing touch. Please heal me physically, spiritually, emotionally, and mentally from all suffering I've been experiencing from the event and the guilt, shame, and self-condemnation.

Pay attention to your body and emotions.
Write out what you are experiencing...

A Prayer of Thanks

Jesus, I thank you, and I receive your healing. Thank you for walking me through forgiving myself. Thank you for taking the heavy garments so I can see the robe of righteousness you gave to me. Help me never to put on those heavy garments again.

Another well done, my friend! Before we move on, go with Jesus to a full-length mirror and check out your robe of righteousness. Look at it in detail. Run back to the mirror and look at it again when satan comes around with his lies and heavy garments. Your robe is too valuable to be covered up. It is stunningly simple and perfectly pure. Just like Jesus. Just like you.

CHAPTER TWENTY-SEVEN

Letting Go

This may be a hard chapter for some; for others, it may be a breeze, but it is something we most likely all struggle with some time in life—letting go of anger and resentment toward God. I would be remiss not to address the times we have held God to our standards and held offenses against Him for allowing and not protecting us or others from harm, disease, and death. With these offenses come the same toxic emotions of anger, resentment, and bitterness that we have toward others who harm us.

Have you ever asked, "Why me, God?" or wondered why He allowed something to happen? I have. We are wired for peace, and when we do not have all the answers, we reason that if we can wrap our finite minds around *why* it happened, or why God did not intervene or prevent it, maybe we would have an answer and be better able to cope with the situation. After all, God is all knowing; shouldn't He have the answer and tell us? Consciously or unconsciously, we demand to know why.

When we do not get answers, justice, or both, we start harboring ill will toward the One who could have done something, healed someone, prevented something, but chose not to. With ill will comes toxic emotions and negative thoughts that take up valuable space in our hearts and minds. Toxic emotions such as anger blind us to the truth that God, in His sovereignty, does not really owe us an answer, even though He has one. Instead of running to Him for comfort and help in our pain, we choose to disconnect, lash out, or give Him the silent treatment. We allow bitterness to brood deep within us and let that bitterness feed the resentment we soon feel toward Him for permitting something terrible or for not preventing it in the first place. We begin to see God as cold, hard, and untrustworthy. We feel like we cannot trust Him and doubt His goodness toward us. As time goes on, we find ourselves blaming Him for other events, too. We may even buy into the lie that He caused the pain to punish us. As we spiral deeper down into the pit of unforgiveness and further close off our hearts to God and others, the devil is laughing. We have fallen right into the web of lies in which he has ensnared us, lies that go against the true nature of our Heavenly Father. Lies that say,

God doesn't really care about you.

God doesn't hear you; who do you think you are anyway?

God didn't answer your prayers; you must be doing something wrong.

If God is love, He wouldn't have allowed this to happen to you or your loved one.

Have you heard those or similar lies? The devil wants to drive distance between us and the One who loves us and can help us.

Satan is an accuser. Before God, he accuses us. Before us, he accuses God. (Revelations 12:10)

He wants us to lose sight of the fact that God does not cause evil (James 1:13) and that in Him there is no darkness (1 John 1:5). Satan, the father of lies, wants us to doubt our Heavenly Father's goodness, mercy, and compassion. If we doubt, we will lose confidence that God sees us or wants to take care of us. We will start to question if God is trustworthy or we will think we did something wrong and deserved it as punishment. We will begin to feel like we are alone or unworthy of His love and protection. We will withdraw farther from our Heavenly Father in pain and frustration when all He desires is to pull us into His arms, comfort us, and walk us through the pain to a place of healing and restoration.

When we have not experienced the healing touch of Jesus in painful events, it is easy to focus on the hurt and pain and lose trust in God's love, sovereignty, and ability to heal, restore, and redeem.

God is pained when those he created promote evil and harm others. Someday it will be made right, as justice will be served (2 Thessalonians 1:6). In the meantime, He provides a way to healing and freedom through Jesus for each one of us. It is His heart's desire for us to live life walking in the fullness of our purpose and in His love.

> *Every gift God freely gives us is good and perfect, streaming down from the Father of lights, who shines from the heavens with no hidden shadow or darkness and is never subject to change. God was delighted to give us birth by the truth of his infallible Word so that we would fulfill his chosen destiny for us and become the favorite ones out of all his creation! (James 1:17, 18; TPT)*

I am thankful God is not subject to change—that He is love and wants the best for His children. He sees the beginning to the end, and for those who love Him, we know He will work out good in all things (Romans 8:28). Jesus is a reflection of the Father. When Jesus came to earth, He was an expression of our Heavenly Father's heart and nature—one who provides comfort, healing, freedom, and restoration. The good news is shared in Isaiah 61 of the Old Testament and again in Luke 4 in the New Testament.

> *The Spirit of the Sovereign Lord is on me because the Lord has anointed me to proclaim good news to the poor. He has sent me to bind up the brokenhearted, to proclaim freedom for the captives and release from darkness for the prisoners, to proclaim the year of the Lord's favor and the day of vengeance of our God, to comfort all who mourn and provide for those who grieve...to bestow on them a crown of beauty instead of ashes, the oil of joy instead of mourning, and a garment of praise instead of a spirit of despair. They will be called oaks of righteousness, a planting of the Lord for the display of his splendor (Isaiah 61:1-3).*

Throughout the Gospels, the goodness of God is on display as Jesus healed the sick, cleansed those with diseases, and brought freedom to tormented souls. He commanded his disciples to do the same as they also had received forgiveness, healing, and freedom.

> *"Proclaim this message: 'The kingdom of heaven has come near.' Heal the sick, raise the dead, cleanse those who have leprosy, drive out demons. Freely you have received; freely give"* *(Matthew 10:8).*

God is a God of justice, and one of recompense (Isaiah 35:4). He does not expect us to understand the whys, He simply asks us to trust that He is for us and not against us and that His plans and purposes will work out better than what we can ever dream or imagine, regardless of how much pain we endure (Jeremiah 29:11, Ephesians 3:19-20).

God wants us to trust in His unwavering love for us and that He can redeem all things when we allow Him access to them. It is time to quit blaming God and start trusting Him instead of believing the lies the devil whispers in our ears. It is time we quit holding God to our standards and expectations and let go of the anger and bitterness that has accumulated in our hearts because we feel He did or did not do something.

Jesus once whispered to my troubled heart, "Father God did not allow anything in your life that could not be healed and redeemed for His glory." That day, I made a choice; I chose to trust Him at His Word and relinquished my right to know all the details and control all the outcomes. Since that time, Jesus has walked me through letting go of the anger I held against God for not protecting me when I was little. He has also helped me let go of the disappointment I felt toward Him because He did not heal and allowed those I loved and prayed for to die, and the list goes on.

Some "letting go's" have been easier than others, but all have been worth it. When we let go, our hearts and hands are free for Him to place something better in them. I invite you to join me and make a choice today to let go of your right to understand and simply take His hand.

> *The Lord is my shepherd; I lack nothing. He makes me lie down in green pastures, he leads me beside quiet waters, he refreshes my soul. He guides me along the right paths for his name's sake. Even though I walk through the darkest valley, I will fear no evil, for you are with*

me; your rod and your staff, they comfort me. You prepare a table before me in the presence of my enemies. You anoint my head with oil; my cup overflows. Surely your goodness and love will follow me all the days of my life, and I will dwell in the house of the Lord forever (Psalm 23).

To encourage your heart, I offer the story of my friend Julie, who once viewed God as the "take away" God. From the viewpoint of a three-year-old child, He took away her dad. From the viewpoint of a seventeen-year-old teenager, He took away her cherished Grandma. From the viewpoint of a thirty-one-year-old daughter, He took away her mom.

The only piece I had left of my dad was his watch that my mom gave me. I kept it and cherished it, wondering what my dad would have been like had he lived and what our relationship would've been like had he not been taken from me. Growing up, I had this fear, this dread, that if God looked at me, He would take my life away too. The faulty belief in my mind was that God was to be feared and that He was the "take-away" God. After my mom passed away from cancer, I went through an abyss of sorrow and despair. Yet again, God had taken someone away from me. The pastor tried to tell me that God would make something good of it all, but I felt like an orphan abandoned by sickness, death, and God Himself.

Fourteen years after my mom passed, I received my first diagnosis of breast cancer. It was through that journey that I began to draw close to Jesus. He was like a brother to me, easy to relate to, and He began to win my trust. Eight years after that, at the age of fifty-three, what was left of my world began to crumble underneath my feet. This time the diagnosis was Stage Three, and I found myself living under the words spoken over me of "if." I again mourned; this time, the loss of my breasts. I had lost those I loved, and now I was losing pieces of myself. My faith was at a crisis level, and I wanted to walk away from it thinking, *God never hears my prayers anyway.* However, Jesus wouldn't let me walk away so easily, and He challenged me to go all in with Him.

During my second round of cancer, Jesus began slowly revealing to me that I had a deep root of bitterness toward God. As He gently took me back to past experiences, He began to show me where my belief that God was a "take-away" God first occurred. It had started when I lost my dad at an early age. One day, Jesus had the audacity to ask me to give my brother dad's watch! I struggled. I argued. Finally, I chose to trust Jesus with everything I was and everything I had. I gave the watch to my brother on his birthday. Jesus knew it was a sacrifice for me; it was me letting go of another piece, the only piece, I had of my earthly father. As I let go of the watch, I grabbed onto Jesus with both hands.

Jesus knew I also needed to let go of the bitterness and resentment I had toward God in my heart. One day, when Kimberly asked Jesus to take me back to a memory, I found myself back at the house where I had lived when my dad was alive. I was around the age of three and Father God was sitting in the chair that my dad had bought my mom right before he died. Jesus sat me on God's lap. My three-year-old self wasn't afraid of God, and it felt comforting and somehow healing to be back in my childhood. Kimberly felt God wanted to "give me back" something. She had no idea what I had been through or my viewpoint of God. As she said those words, Father God reached into His pocket and pulled out my dad's watch, the watch I had given to my brother a few weeks earlier. He placed it in my little hands, and I broke. As I sobbed out my sorrow, I forgave God for taking my dad, for allowing him to die from the heart attack. I forgave Him for not saving my Grandma, and for not healing my mom.

In those precious moments, something shifted in my heart and mind. God *saw* me and *loved* me. He cared about everything I had experienced. That day, my viewpoint of God went from being the "take-away" God to the "give-back" God. Since then, Father God has continued to heal me and show me who He is as my *loving* Heavenly Father."

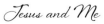

Julie shared with me that since that day in God's lap, she is no longer afraid of Him. She is happy to climb up in His lap and receive the love He showers upon her. Your Heavenly Father wants to do that for you, too.

Exercise: Letting Go of Resentment Toward God

Time: 15-20 Minutes

Physical Place: A quiet place away from distractions

Materials: Journal or paper and pen or pencil

Your Heavenly Father loves you, wants you, and adores you. He does not want anything keeping you from His embrace. Jesus' finished work on the cross gives you full access at all times. When we are upset with God or hold things against Him because we do not understand why He allowed something to happen or did not do something we asked, it only hurts us. His heart is for us to come to Him and trust Him with our all—especially with the things we do not understand.

There are times we may not even realize we have resentment or bitterness toward God until Jesus points it out. This exercise will take 15 to 20 minutes depending on how much Jesus shows you. You can do this exercise in your Secret Place or invite Jesus to be with you in your physical space. When you feel His peace and Presence, continue.

OPENING PRAYER

Jesus, I thank you for being with me now. I surrender my spirit, soul, and body to the Holy Spirit and ask you to release your Peace within me and around me.

I trust you to show me where I may be holding anger and resentment against God the Father. Guard my heart and mind and bind up any unholy spirits that may try to interfere with our time together or this exercise.

When you are at peace and feel safe with Jesus, continue by asking Jesus to reveal where you may be upset with God.

Jesus, will you reveal to me if there is an area where I'm upset with God?

Jesus may tell you, bring an experience back to your mind, or He may ask you to return to a memory with Him. If you see or hear more than one thing, ask Jesus on which one you should focus.

What does Jesus say or reveal to you?

Write out what you are upset with God about and why you are upset with Him.

"God, I am upset/mad/angry at you because

_____."

Vocalize to God the impact it had on your life.

"God, when you allowed this to happen, it
(What impact has it had on you and your life?)

_____."

Talk to Jesus about any emotions or negative thoughts you are experiencing from the event.

Jesus, please reveal to me any toxic emotions or negative thoughts I'm experiencing from the event.

What does Jesus say or reveal to you?

Hand your negative thoughts and toxic emotions to Jesus. Visualize doing so and see Him taking them from you.

Jesus, I give you all the negative thoughts and toxic emotions: the anger, the resentment, the bitterness (add any other emotions you feel). I give them all to you.

What do your negative thoughts and emotions look like?

What does Jesus do with the negative thoughts
and emotions that you give Him?

You are doing great. Now it is time to tell Heavenly Father you are sorry and ask Jesus to cleanse all the places that have been affected. During this part, Jesus may want to take you to your Heavenly Father. If so, do not be afraid; Jesus is with you. Your Heavenly Father loves to see you, and is not mad or disappointed in you. He is thrilled that you are letting go to grab His hand.

Jesus, I don't want to be upset with God anymore. I ask you and Father God to forgive me for holding things against God and for my anger, resentment, and bitterness that I've felt toward God because (state why you're angry with God)

_____.

Forgive me for the bad thoughts I've had against you, God. Thank you for your unfailing love and enduring grace and mercy. Thank you for forgiving me. I receive your forgiveness.

What does Jesus and/or Father God say or do?

Ask Jesus to cleanse the ill will from your heart and fill those places with more love.

Jesus, I ask you to cleanse the ill will toward God from my heart and cleanse each area of my spirit, soul, and body from the negative thoughts and toxic emotions attached to the event.

Please fill those places with more of your love and the love of my Heavenly Father.

Journal what you are seeing and experiencing
during the time of cleansing and filling...

When you are ready to continue, ask Jesus if you believe any lies or faulty beliefs from that experience. If so, write them in the section below.

Jesus, please bring to my attention any lies or faulty beliefs I believe from this experience. Do I believe any lies about...

God?

You (Jesus)?

Myself?

Someone else?

If Jesus shows you something, it is important to tell Him and Father God that you are sorry for making an agreement, knowingly or unknowingly, with each lie, and to renounce and break agreement with the lie. We want to dig up the root of each lie and plant His truth.

Jesus: Thank you for revealing the lie(s) and faulty belief(s) to me! I want your truth planted instead.

I ask you to forgive me for taking agreement with (name lie or faulty belief), and I receive your forgiveness. I now renounce and break all agreements I knowingly or unknowingly made with the lie(s) and faulty belief(s).

Jesus, what truth do you want to plant in my heart and mind now?

What truth does Jesus share with you? (Write it in the prayer below.)

Ask Jesus to plant the truth deep in your heart and mind.

Jesus, I thank you for planting your truth that (state truth)

Please plant the truth deep in my heart and in my mind. Water it with your love and with your living Word. Help me to run to you and My Heavenly Father when I get hurt. Thank you for your love for me.

It is time to use your authority in Jesus Christ to let the enemy know he is no longer welcome and has to leave. Say this prayer aloud.

In the name of Jesus Christ, I command any unholy spirits that once had a right because of my offense against God to cease all torment. Jesus and My Heavenly Father have forgiven me. I've forgiven myself too! Jesus has cleansed that area in my heart and filled it with His love. I repent and renounce any past thought or behavior that allowed the unholy spirits to attach in any way.

You no longer have any right to stay, and you must pack your bags and leave now without throwing any tantrums or causing any damage. Go now where Jesus sends you. I now place the cross and blood of Jesus Christ between myself and the unholy spirits that left. You are not welcome back.

Journal anything you experienced during this prayer...

Ask Jesus to heal any place that has been suffering from the experience.

Jesus, I need your healing touch. Please heal me physically, spiritually, emotionally, and mentally from all suffering I've been experiencing from the event.

Pay attention to your body and emotions and journal
what you are experiencing...

Prayer of Thanks

Jesus, I thank you for walking me through letting go of my resentment toward Father God. I receive your grace, your healing, and your love.

Jesus and I are so proud of you! You have accomplished some major heart and soul cleansing. In the next chapter, we will take a more in-depth look into trauma and healing traumatic memories with Jesus.

CHAPTER TWENTY-EIGHT

Walking Through Traumatic Memories with Jesus

No one is exempt from hurt and pain in life. Jesus experienced it as well. I am grateful He stayed the course for us and overcame the powers of darkness so He can help us through our times of pain and darkness. In John 8:12, Jesus shares that He is the light of the world, and those who go with Him will never walk in darkness but will have the light of life. When we walk hand-in-hand with Jesus, we have the Light of Life *with* us bringing to light the places in our lives that He wants to heal at that time.

When we are *with* Him, we are safe and understand that He is who we need Him to be in our past memories and present situations. Because Jesus is the source of light and all truth, we can trust Him to guide us and to be our Rescuer, Deliverer, Healer, Comforter, Redeemer, and Restorer.

I pray that since the time you wrote your name and date at the beginning of Part II, you have encountered Jesus and His love for you in new and profound ways. I pray you have grabbed hold of the nail-scarred hands that hold your past, your present, and your future. When you are hand-in-hand with Jesus, you have the Source Himself, for He is the grace you need at the moment, the air for your next breath, the answer to your questions, the comfort for your hurting heart, and the lamp that lights your way.

As you go through this chapter's exercise, it will be important to let Jesus lead and light each step. He loves you and cares for you—spirit, soul, and body. He wants complete healing and may bring you healing all at once, little-by-little, or through several different means. There are often layers and dimensions to traumatic memories that need to be uncovered carefully and in a particular order; it is important to trust Jesus and His timing. It is okay to uncover and heal one layer at a time, and it is okay to ask others for help. For those who have suffered abuse over long periods of time or those with severe or complex trauma where you experience flashbacks, consider walking through the memory exercise with a Christian therapist or psychologist trained in trauma work. You are not in this alone; Jesus is with you, and so are others.

Hopefully, you have worked your way through the chapters and exercises in the order they were placed and are now familiar with the importance of being attuned with Jesus and experiencing His peace and safety. You have had time in your Secret Place developing a relationship of trust with Jesus as you experience His desire to be with you without judgment. Spending time with Him, you have come to realize that He sees you, hears you, understands what you have been through, and desires to help you. You have become more familiar with His voice and His kind and gentle ways. You have experienced the power and freedom from forgiving others and yourself. You have practiced how to give Jesus your toxic emotions and have allowed Him to cleanse areas in your spirit, soul, and body and fill you with His love and peace. You have learned the importance of uncovering and digging up the roots of lies and faulty beliefs and allowed Jesus to plant His truth. Using your voice, you broke agreements with lies and told the enemy to get lost.

In Chapter 23, *Wired for Peace*, you walked through a memory with Jesus where you asked Him to heal your hurt, cleanse the traumatized neural pathway, and reframe the memory from a place of pain and trauma into a place of peace. Many of the elements introduced in previous exercises will be incorporated in this chapter's exercise; if you skipped over the other chapters and exercises, please go back and work your way through them before walking through this one.

As a reminder, you are uniquely created and have your own unique experiences. Jesus knows each traumatic experience stored in your nonconsciousness mind. He knows what emotions, feelings, and beliefs are tied to each memory, and He knows how and when to take you to the memory. Remember, nothing is insignificant or too big for Jesus.

I have added wording in this exercise's prayer to bind up fear. Fear loves trauma, and we want the regions in your brain and the systems in your body affected by fear to quiet down so that you are able to receive what Jesus has for you. You will also pray for the Holy Spirit and Jesus to correct any imbalance and wiring in your brain that needs to be addressed, as well as heal specific regions of the brain affected by the trauma.[28] Remember, trauma in our context is any experience not processed into a place of peace.

Studies show that trauma alters brain functioning and if not dealt with can affect the brain long-term, especially for those who are suffering from PTSD. A traumatized brain looks different than a non-traumatized brain in three particular regions: The amygdala, which plays a major role in the fight-or-flight response, stays on and becomes over activated while the prefrontal cortex, the thinking center, and the anterior cingulate cortex, the emotion-regulating center, become under activated and shrink in volume.[29] Again, you are wonderfully made, and studies have shown that volume can be regenerated in the hippocampus.[30,31] You will see these areas of the brain and others addressed in the Trauma Healing Prayer section of the exercise.

Statistics for those suffering from significant trauma are high. According to the nonprofit PTSD United, Inc., 70% of U.S. adults have experienced a significant trauma at least once in their lifetime. That equates to 223.4 million people with 20% further developing PTSD. That is 44.7 million people who were or are struggling with PTSD. Estimates also show that one of every nine women develops PTSD, making women twice as likely as men to develop it.[32] Statistics may be high, and you may be one who has suffered significant trauma; but you, my friend, are not a statistic to Jesus. You are loved and personally known by a Savior who came to rescue, heal, and restore that which the enemy meant for harm.

Jesus came to walk the road of healing with you.

I have had the privilege of helping others walk through traumatic memories with Jesus and have watched Him love and heal emotionally, mentally, spiritually, and physically; it is a walk of hope and healing. I encourage you to walk through this exercise with Him time and time again—allowing Jesus to lead and light the way. For those who have faced or are presently facing a life-threatening prognosis, I pray Britt's story brings you hope as you walk your road of healing with Jesus.

In my Secret Place, Jesus and I were fishing (We both love to fish!). His first words to me were, "Let not your 'heart' be troubled." I love those words, as eight months earlier I had open heart surgery to remove a blood clot that ran the length of my body from my ankle into my heart.

The memory Jesus took me to was the moment the doctors told me the news. As I lay in the hospital bed listening to the doctors tell me I might not make it, I felt fear and death encircle me. When I looked for Jesus in the memory, He was right by my bed, holding my hand and smiling! He said, "I won't let the spirit of death take you." As Jesus stood next to me speaking those words, I knew I wouldn't die from the life-threatening blood clot. Calmness and the peace of Jesus replaced the anxiety and fear.

Jesus revealed that I was carrying concern and fear over what would happen to my family if I was to die—personally and financially. I handed all I felt to Him—the fear, the concern, and the responsibility. I asked Him to cleanse the areas in me that had been affected. With one hand, He began removing black stuff from me (the fear, concern, anxiety), while at the same time, with His other hand, putting His light in me (love, peace, and joy). His light finally replaced all the darkness. I then gave all the people I was concerned about to Jesus. His arms began to stretch around them (like a Stretch Armstrong toy), and I knew He had them and would take care of them.

The person I needed to forgive was me. My previous lifestyle choices had been part of what led to the health crisis, which also involved them finding kidney cancer. My choices had brought on some of my own trauma. No longer did I want the guilt, shame, or self-condemnation. I gave it all to Jesus and asked Him to forgive me. He did and went on to share that during those months where my life hung in the balance, I had tried to rebuke death in my own flesh. I believed the lie that I could do it in my own power and had this feeling of invincibility. When Jesus showed me this, I saw myself holding a dingy black beat-up shield. I handed it to Jesus and thanked Him for revealing to me the lie I had subconsciously believed. He smiled as He handed me a new shield—a large, white one trimmed in gold. He told me to use His "shield of righteousness" when the enemy comes back around whispering non-stop in my ear, "This is your last heartbeat. This is your last breath."

I—trying to fight death by my own power—had also left room for doubt and deception to sneak into my thinking. When I broke agreement with the lie that I could do it in my strength, I made sure that I kicked out fear, doubt, and deception on their backsides as I prayed the prayer to let them know they no longer had a right. With Jesus beside me, I stand in the truth that nothing can stand against what Jesus speaks.

When I think back on that day, I now see Jesus in the hospital room standing next to me and me holding *His* shield of righteousness. Each day I thank Him for my breath, my heartbeat, and the Words of life He continually speaks over me.

> *As for God, his way is perfect; The Lord's word is flawless; he shields all who take refuge in Him (Psalm 18:30).*

> *Now, O Lord GOD, You are God, and Your words are truth, and You have promised this good thing to Your servant (2 Samuel 7:28; NLT).*

Exercise: Processing Traumatic Memories with Jesus

Time: 30-60 Minutes

Physical Place: A quiet place away from distractions

Materials: Journal or paper and pen or pencil

In the chapter, *Wired for Peace*, we covered how the nonconscious mind is the place where long-term memories, ingrained behaviors and habits, and deep-seated emotions reside. It is home to beliefs and is the core of who you are. When Jesus brings up a painful memory, He wants to heal the emotions, thought patterns, protective measures, and beliefs tied to that experience.

From the moment a "first occurrence" trauma occurs, events after that get filtered through the lens of that first occurrence. First occurrences are where seeds get planted and where roots take hold. Early-childhood and prolonged trauma can cause strong roots that grow deep. Jesus wants to get to root issues in your heart and soul because they are affecting your identity.

Jesus knows if and when you are mentally and emotionally ready to step into a past experience. For me, He sometimes took me to seemingly insignificant events and worked His way to the core of a painful first occurrence. Once we got to the first occurrence, healing happened at the core, with the uprooting of lies and planting of His truth. Other times, He performed significant healing upfront with the untangling of lies and faulty beliefs taking place over time as they were intertwined with other areas of my life that still needed healing.

Holding His hand and letting Him lead the way is an important reminder. He loves you and knows what is best for you. He knows where to take you to bring you into healing and wholeness. Sometimes, it involves walking through past pain that you would rather not uncover. However, just because it is buried deep, does not mean that it is not affecting you and your identity. It is. I know, from experience. I also know the healing work that can be done when Jesus is trusted with the pain.

Healing is a journey of trust, one you do together—in relationship.

This is a journey where Jesus allows you to be a part of the process, where you are empowered to make choices to no longer be a victim of trauma, but an overcomer in Him.

> *I have told you these things, so that in me you may have peace. In this world, you will have trouble. But take heart! I have overcome the world (John 16:33).*

Returning to a significant traumatic memory can sometimes feel like it is in the present. Your brain wants to protect you and your "rapid response system" kicks on, wanting you to either (1) fight to save your life or (2) get far away from it. Often, you will have the urge to shove the memory back down and not look at it. To help stay in the present and be able to walk through the memory with Jesus, I want to share two techniques that you can physically do to help the reasoning center of your prefrontal cortex stay turned on so you will be aware that the traumatic event happened in the past and is not reoccurring in the present. When you know you are okay in the present, you will be better able to process the experience with Jesus.

Deep Breathing

The first technique is deep breathing. God designed us to experience His peace in our spirit, mind, and body. He created us in a way to be physically able to notice stress and work with how He designed us; helping us move from a place of stress into a place of peace physiologically. He really has thought of everything! Deep breathing relieves stress and anxiety due to its physiological effect on the nervous system. Breathing deeply slowly triggers the parasympathetic nervous system causing the body to secrete hormones to decrease blood pressure and heart rate, helping bring about a relaxation response.[33] It is the opposite of fear's fight-or-flight stress response.[34] One easy-to-remember breathing technique is the 5-2-5 technique. Practice it before starting this exercise to help you relax. If you are a person who likes to use words instead of numbers, I have put in some words that are helpful to say.

1. Take a long, slow breath in through your nose, filling your lower lungs first, then your upper lungs. As you inhale in your mind, count to five or say "Thank you for your peace."

2. Hold your breath and count to two or say, "I receive."

3. Exhale slowly in a sigh through your open mouth. As you sigh, count to five or say, "Thank you for your love." As you let out your breath, focus on relaxing the muscles in your face, jaw, shoulders, and stomach.

A Tangible Reminder

Another way to help your reasoning center stay open is to have something tangible to remind you that you are in the present moment—safe and not physically back in the memory.[35] You can touch the chair you are sitting in and say, "I'm okay. I'm safe." You may find it helpful to write out a verse and hold it in your hands as you walk through the exercise. One of my favorite verses is Isaiah 43:1 (GNT).

> *The Lord who created you says, "Do not be afraid—I will save you. I have called you by name—you are mine."*

These are other verses you may find helpful to write out and hold.

> *Peace I leave with you; my peace I give you. I do not give to you as the world gives. Do not let your hearts be troubled and do not be afraid (John 14:27).*

> *Yet I am not alone, for my Father is with me. "I have told you these things, so that in me you may have peace. In this world, you will have trouble. But take heart! I have overcome the world" (John 16:32, 33).*

If you start to feel anxious, you can take actions in the natural to help you override anxiety and stay attuned to Jesus so He can continue to walk you through the Pain-Processing Pathway successfully. If feelings of anxiety arise, practice deep breathing and focus on a verse you are holding in your hand.

Set aside 30 to 60 minutes for this exercise; the exercise may take you more or less time depending on the memory and what Jesus wants to walk through with you. The exercise is in sections, so if you need to take a break, try to do so at the end of a section. Most of the elements you have learned in the previous exercises are incorporated. Since you have learned them and practiced them, only a few teaching tips are included; if you skipped over the other chapters and exercises, please go back and work your way through them before walking through this one.

It is important, especially for this exercise, to start in a place of peace with Jesus. You will start in the Secret Place and spend time with Him, getting attuned to Him, and experiencing His love and peace.

Start with the opening prayer of surrender and cleansing.

OPENING PRAYER

Jesus: Thank you for never leaving me or forsaking me. Thank you for the healing in my life that you have already brought to me.

I surrender my spirit, soul, and body to the Holy Spirit. I ask you to cleanse my physical and spiritual senses and attune them to you through the Holy Spirit. I give you my mind, my imagination, and all my memories. Cleanse and purify them from all things that are not of you. Help me clearly see and perceive you and all that you are going to reveal to me in this exercise.

I ask you to re-establish any connection that needs to be repaired between the hemispheres of my brain. If anything was disconnected that needs reconnecting, please reconnect it now. If there is anything wired incorrectly, please wire it correctly so that I can process this memory correctly with you. Please correct any chemical, electrical, and magnetic communication paths and restore them to their proper balance.

Thank you for your Presence of Peace. I ask that you surround me with it now, and quiet all distractions and other voices except yours. Guard my mind and heart and bind up any unholy spirits that may try to interfere with our time together and this exercise. I claim in your name, Jesus, fear has no place here. Thank you, Jesus, for your goodness, your faithfulness, and your love for me. Thank you for being with me each step of the way, guiding me into light and truth.

Visualize your Secret Place and invite Jesus to come and join you there.

189

Jesus, I invite you to join me in our Secret Place.

When Jesus comes to you, take time to enjoy His Presence and the love and peace that He brings.

Jesus, is there anything you want to tell me before you take me back to a memory?

What does Jesus say?

How do you feel emotionally and physically?

RECALLING A MEMORY WITH JESUS

When you are ready, ask Jesus to bring to your mind a memory He wants to highlight. Following the template below, ask Jesus to go with you into the memory so that you can see Him there. If at any time, during the memory work, you search for Jesus and do not see Him or you feel uncomfortable, return to your Secret Place and talk with Jesus about it. You are on this journey *with* Jesus. He is your safe place in the memory, so it is important to know He is with you during each piece of the exercise.

Jesus, please bring back to my mind a memory you want to show me.

It is usually the first thought or memory that comes to your mind. Remember, nothing is insignificant. See where it leads with Him. If several memories come up, ask Jesus which one He wants you to focus on.

Where is Jesus in the memory?

What is Jesus doing?

What does Jesus say to you?

Spend some time with Jesus and journal what you can remember of the memory to help you identify possible triggers.

What event is occurring?

In the memory, where are you and what are you doing?

What are you hearing, seeing, smelling, tasting, experiencing physically?

What age are you or what time of life are you in?
For example: age 6, junior high, just married, et cetera.

What emotions are you feeling? *Emotions coming up may be loneliness, sadness, anger, fear, or other negative emotions.*

What does Jesus say or reveal to you
about the experience and the emotions you are feeling?

FREEDOM OF FORGIVENESS

We do not want toxins leaking from our heart or the enemy having any right to camp out, so now it is time to ask Jesus if you need to forgive anyone or yourself.

Jesus, please show me if there is a person(s) attached to this memory that I need to forgive. Do I need to forgive...

Person(s)?

Myself?

God or Jesus?

Below are forgiveness prayers for others, yourself, and God. I find it helpful to say these prayers aloud; doing so helps your mind agree with what you are doing in your heart. Ask Jesus to stand beside you in the memory as you forgive.

FORGIVING OTHERS:

The prayer below will walk you through addressing the offender, forgiving, and *releasing* him or her to Jesus as well as *relinquishing* your right to make the person pay. You will have a voice as you address (1) what the offender did to you, (2) how it affected you and your life, and (3) how it made you feel.

(Name of the offender)_____, what you did to me was wrong.

When you (List the wrongs done to you.)...

_____.

it (State how it affected you and your life.)...

_____.

Your actions/words made me feel...

_____.

I'm choosing now, with Jesus' help, to forgive you as Jesus forgave me. I forgive you for the wrong you did to me, how you made me feel, and the effects it had on my spirit, soul, and body.

Jesus, I ask you to forgive (name of offender) _____ for (his / her) offenses against me, for how (his / her) actions made me feel, and how the actions/words affected me.

Help open the heart of _____ so you can heal (his / her) heart also. Bless _____ and work in (his / her) life in a redemptive way.

Jesus, I release _____ to you, and I relinquish my right to make (him / her) pay by getting revenge or bringing punishment upon (him / her). Jesus, I'm putting _____ in your hands now. Please walk _____ out of my heart.

Walk the person over to Jesus. Jesus will walk the person out of your heart. When Jesus returns (He always has a big smile on His face when He comes back to me.), give Jesus permission to clean out and cleanse that area of your heart where your offender once resided along with any unholy effects and toxic emotions.

Jesus, my heart is yours. Forgive me for the bad thoughts and toxic emotions I harbored in my heart and mind against my offender. Please cleanse that space in my heart and mind now.

Clean out all toxic emotions (anger, hurt, bitterness, revenge, et cetera). If I've put up any walls in this space, please remove them so this space is open and free to be filled with your love. Jesus, I ask that you cleanse and purify me from all the unholy effects (name of offender's) _____ transgressions against me have had on my spirit, my soul, and my body.

What is Jesus doing?

What are you feeling?

When Jesus is done cleansing that area, ask Him to fill it with His love and peace.

Jesus, please fill that clean space in my heart now with your love and peace.

NEEDING FORGIVENESS FROM SOMEONE YOU HURT:

Ask Jesus if there is a person you need to ask for forgiveness.

⬥━━⬥●⬥●⬥━━⬥

Jesus, is there anyone's forgiveness I need to ask for in relation to the experience?

If Jesus shows you anyone, you can use this prayer while picturing the person there with you and Jesus. It is also a good template to use should Jesus ask you to go in person to apologize and ask for forgiveness.

⬥━━⬥●⬥●⬥━━⬥

(Name of person you hurt) _____, I'm sorry for...(List actions or words against the person you hurt.) _____

I'm sorry for the impact my actions and words had on your heart and life. What I did was wrong, please forgive me. I pray that Jesus will heal the wounds I've caused you.

If there is a response from the person you are forgiving, journal it here...

Ask Jesus to heal the person of your hurt and to bless the person.

⬥━━⬥●⬥●⬥━━⬥

Jesus, will you please take away the harmful effects my actions had on (the person you hurt) _____. Cleanse (his / her) spirit, soul, and body with your cleansing blood and heal (him / her). Fill those places where I wounded _____ with your love and peace. Thank you, Jesus, for caring about us all. I ask you to bless _____ now.

FORGIVING YOURSELF:

The prayer below is for you if Jesus reveals the need to forgive yourself in any way and let yourself out of your heart; no more wearing garments of guilt, shame, and self-condemnation over your robe of righteousness.

Jesus, I'm sorry for the wrong I did that hurt _____ and I'm sorry for carrying all this guilt and shame. Will you please forgive me?

What does Jesus say or do?

Hand Jesus the garments of guilt, shame, self-condemnation, and all the negative emotions and thoughts that go with them. If you have a hard time doing so, ask Jesus to help you.

Jesus, I don't want to carry the guilt, shame, or self-condemnation any longer. I release all these heavy garments and negative feelings and thoughts to you and relinquish all rights to punish myself in any way.

What does Jesus do with the garments, feelings, and thoughts?

What does Jesus say to you?

Jesus, thank you for taking my guilt and shame and the condemnation I had toward myself. It no longer belongs to me. I ask you now to cleanse that area in my heart and all the areas in my life that were affected by it. Please fill those places now with your love, acceptance, and peace.

What do you see Jesus doing?

What are you experiencing?

Let the "you" in your heart know you are free, and ask Jesus to reunite the once locked-up you with who you are today.

———————————◆◆◆◆◆◆———————————

(Your name) _____, you are free! As of (date _____),
the garments of guilt, shame, and self-condemnation no longer belong to
you. Jesus, now that I am no longer locked up in my heart, please reunite
that part of me with who I am today.

Take a few minutes and journal what you are experiencing
spiritually, emotionally, mentally, physically …

ADDRESSING ANGER AND RESENTMENT TOWARD GOD:

Ask Jesus if you are holding anything against Him or God in relation to that memory. If He reveals anything, write out what you are upset with God or Jesus about and why you are upset with Him.

"God, I am upset/mad/angry at you because _____."

Vocalize to God the impact it had on your life.

"God, when you allowed this to happen, it...(What impact has it had on you and your life?) _____."

Talk to Jesus about any emotions or negative thoughts you are experiencing from the event.

Jesus, please reveal to me any toxic emotions or negative thoughts I'm experiencing from the event.

What does Jesus say or reveal to you?

Hand your negative thoughts and toxic emotions to Jesus. Visualize doing so and see Him taking them from you.

Jesus, I give you all the negative thoughts and toxic emotions: the anger, the resentment, the bitterness (any other emotions you feel). I give them all to you.

What do your negative thoughts and emotions look like?

What does Jesus do with the negative thoughts
and emotions you are giving Him?

You are doing great. Now it is time to tell Heavenly Father you are sorry and ask Jesus to cleanse all the places that have been affected. During this part, Jesus may want to take you to your Heavenly Father. If so, do not be afraid; Jesus is with you. Your Heavenly Father loves to see you, and is not mad or disappointed in you. He is thrilled that you are letting go to grab His hand.

Jesus, I don't want to be upset with God anymore. I ask you and Father God to forgive me for holding things against God and for my anger, resentment, and bitterness that I've felt toward God because (State why you're angry with God.)

Forgive me for the bad thoughts I've had against you, God. Thank you for your unfailing love and enduring grace and mercy. Thank you for forgiving me. I receive your forgiveness.

What does Jesus and/or Father God say or do?

Ask Jesus to cleanse the ill will from your heart and fill those places with more love.

Jesus, I ask you to cleanse the ill will toward God from my heart and cleanse each area of my spirit, soul, and body from the negative thoughts and toxic emotions attached to the event.

Please fill those places with more of your love and the love of my Heavenly Father.

Journal what you are seeing and experiencing
during the time of cleansing and filling...

EXCHANGING & CLEANSING OF EMOTIONS

Go back and review the emotions you listed when Jesus and you walked through the recalled memory. Are there any that you have not addressed through the forgiveness exercises? If so, when you are ready, let Jesus know you want to give Him any remaining emotion(s) you are feeling from the memory in exchange for His peace and love.

Jesus, I don't want to carry the emotion(s) of _____
inside of me any longer. I'm giving the emotion(s) to you.

Picture the emotion(s) in your hands, hand it to Jesus, and see Him taking it from you.

What does your emotion(s) look like?

What does Jesus do with the emotion(s)?

Take a few moments and ask Jesus if there are any additional emotions He wants you to give Him at this time. If there are, hand them to Him.

Journal any other emotions...

When you have finished handing the emotions of the memory to Jesus, ask Him to cleanse the areas where they settled in your spirit, soul, and body and to fill those areas with His love and peace. Visualize Jesus cleansing and filling.

Jesus, thank you for taking the feelings of _____ that came with this memory. I ask you to cleanse any area in my spirit, soul, and body where the emotion(s) settled and fill those places with your love and your peace.

Journal anything you are seeing or experiencing...

REFRAMING THE MEMORY WITH JESUS

When you are ready to move on, ask Jesus to reframe the memory for you. This will be the new memory that you remember; one with Him in it and you at peace. Describe as many details as possible.

Thank you, Jesus, for helping me through the memory thus far. Will you please reframe it for me now so that it is a memory filled with you and your love and peace?

In the memory, where is Jesus at with you?

What is Jesus doing?

What is your reframed memory; how is the memory now different?

Talk to Jesus about the reframed memory
and journal what He shares with you...

You are doing wonderful! When you are ready, continue. Jesus wants to dig up any lies and correct faulty beliefs so you can walk in your true self and fulfill your destiny.

UNCOVERING LIES & FAULTY BELIEFS AND BREAKING AGREEMENT WITH THEM

We can have faulty belief systems from believing a lie in the midst of trauma. Ask Jesus if you believe any lies from the experience. If so, write the lies in the section below.

———————————◆—●■●—■●—————————————

Jesus, please bring to my attention any lies I believe from the past experience. Do I believe any lies about...

The person(s) who hurt me?

Myself?

You (Jesus) or Father God?

If Jesus showed you something, tell Him and Father God you are sorry for agreeing, knowingly or unknowingly, with each lie. It is important to also

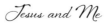

renounce and break agreement with each one. Say the following prayer for each lie.

Jesus: Thank you for revealing the lie to me. I'm sorry for taking agreement with the lie that (state the lie) _____

I ask you to forgive me, and I receive your forgiveness. I now renounce and break all agreements that I knowingly or unknowingly made with the lie.

Now ask Jesus to reveal His truth and let Him plant that deep in your heart and mind.

Jesus, what is your truth? Write the truth that Jesus shares with you in the prayer below.

Jesus, thank you for planting your truth that (write truth) _____

Please plant the truth deep in my heart and in my mind. Water it with your love and with your living Word. Please help me run to you and My Heavenly Father when I get hurt. Thank you for your love for me.

Journal anything you are seeing or experiencing...

KICKING OUT THE ENEMY

Time to tell the enemy he is no longer welcome and use your voice to tell any unholy spirits attached to the experience they have to pack their bags and leave. You will also repent and renounce any thought or behavior that was done in the past that may have allowed the unholy spirits to attach. Remember to say this prayer aloud.

In the name of Jesus Christ, I command any unholy spirits that once had a right from the hurt, trauma, and any offense to cease all torment and harm.

I've forgiven those who needed forgiveness and Jesus has cleansed those areas in my heart and filled it with His love. He has reframed the memory and moved it from a place of fear and trauma to a place of peace. You cannot camp out on unforgiveness or the hurt or wounding any longer. I repent and renounce any past thought or behavior that allowed unholy spirits to attach in any way. You no longer have any right to stay, and you must pack your bags and leave now without throwing any tantrums or causing any damage. Go now where Jesus sends you.

I now place the cross and blood of Jesus Christ between myself and the unholy spirits that left. You are not welcome back!

Journal anything you experienced during this prayer...

PRAYER FOR HEALING OF BRAIN/TRAUMA

For the rest of the exercise, I invite you to go back to your Secret Place with Jesus or to the pool of water by the waterfall and soak in Father God's love.

During the following prayer, you will ask Jesus to cleanse any residual toxic thoughts or negative emotions, wash out the old neural pathway of the original memory, remove the triggers that were set up with it, repair any remaining damage in your brain from the trauma and chemical cascades, and firmly establish your reframed memory—the one where you are now with Him experiencing His peace.

Picture Jesus in front of you as you say this prayer, and ask to see what He is doing as the Holy Spirit works within you.

Jesus, please cleanse my spirit, soul, and body of any and all remaining negative thoughts and toxic emotions attached to this memory and fill those places with your love and peace.

If there are still any places in my brain that need repair from the trauma, I ask you to repair them now. Please cleanse the memory's old neural pathways and remove all the triggers that were set up in my senses and along the neural pathways at the time of the original experience.

Bring peace to my brain and the neural pathways and remove all trauma and any fear-based reactions that cause me to stay in fight-or-flight mode from this memory. Please correct any damage done from long-term trauma to my amygdala, thalamus, hippocampus, anterior cingulate cortex, and prefrontal cortex. Reset them to your original design—on earth in me as it is in Heaven. Please balance all chemical, electrical, and magnetic communication paths and restore them to their proper limits so I can be at peace and function as you intended.

Thank you, Jesus, for the work you and the Holy Spirit are doing within my body, soul, and spirit. I receive your healing and peace to my brain and all systems attached to this memory.

Please establish my reframed memory with you so that I can recall the reframed memory in a place of peace. Thank you for your Presence and for walking me through the memory and bringing it from a place of trauma into a place of peace.

Journal what you are seeing/experiencing...

What is Jesus doing?

What are you experiencing physically, emotionally, or mentally?

Spend more time soaking in His love and peace.

PRAYER FOR HEALING OF SPIRIT, SOUL, BODY

Ask Jesus to heal any place that has been suffering in your spirit, soul, or body from any wounding, trauma, offense, toxic emotions and negative thoughts that were related to the original memory.

Jesus, please heal me from any physical, mental, and emotional suffering that I've been experiencing from the original memory. Will you please let me see what you are doing while the Holy Spirit is working within me?

What is Jesus doing?

What are you experiencing physically, emotionally, or mentally?

A PRAYER OF THANKS

Jesus, I bless what you have done and what you are continuing to do in my spirit, soul, and body. I receive your healing. Thank you for your great love for me, for seeing me, for listening to me, for being my guiding light. I love you. Thank you for restoring my heart and walking me farther down the path into my destiny.

You and Jesus have accomplished some beautiful heart-and-soul work. After each measure of healing, I encourage you to spend extra time with Jesus in the Secret Place. Soak in His love, give your heart time to recover, and give your new roots of truth time to take hold. Jesus will let you know when it is time to take another step forward into more healing. In the meantime, protect your healing and the truth He planted in your heart and mind. Let your new roots grow deep until they become firmly established in His love for you; so

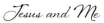

established that when the enemy tries to get you to doubt the healing you received, your worth, or your identity, you will not be swayed or uprooted. The next chapter will give you some helpful ways to help you stand firm in what Jesus has done for you and who you are in Him.

CHAPTER TWENTY-NINE

Protect Your Healing Progress

During my healing journey, faulty beliefs were uprooted, and truths were planted. With each healing, Jesus revealed to me more of my true identity and who He designed me to be. He had a lot of ground to uncover to get to the root of the victim mentality that had developed from the belief that I was powerless and that all I could do was "stay silent and do nothing." That root had been growing since I was a little girl and had a firm hold affecting other areas in my life. It was affecting my destiny.

It was a lengthy journey to get to that first occurrence root, but so worth it. I am thankful Jesus is faithful and never gave up on me. Layer by layer, He moved away the dirt that once held that root firm, and in His perfect timing, carefully dug it up and showed me how the enemy used trauma and fear to silence my voice and make me feel powerless. Once Jesus revealed the root of where I first believed the lie, the freedom flowed afterward. I surrendered it all to Him, forgave those I still needed to forgive, and broke the agreement with the lie.

No longer am I a powerless victim intimidated to "stay silent and do nothing." I am a victor, with a powerful voice to bring others into the arms of Jesus to walk a personal journey of healing and restoration. When we take the hand of Jesus and trust Him to guide us through the pain and trauma into a place of healing and peace, He is faithful to complete the good work He started in each of us (Philippians 1:6).

After each major healing and planting of truth, Jesus allowed time for the new truth to take hold. He did not seem to be in a big hurry to clean me up. In His kindness and wisdom, He gave me time to heal and gave the "roots of truth" time to become firmly established in His love. As the new roots took hold and new thought patterns took shape, the enemy always returned, testing me, taunting me, wanting me to fall back into faulty thinking, trying to entice me to pick up the old lies and renew my pact with them. Jesus used that time to teach me how to protect my roots of truth and how to use my voice. That time of testing strengthened my faith and trust in Jesus—and in myself. As I chose to focus on Jesus and His healing work in my life, new beliefs and behaviors became ingrained in my soul. Self-protective walls came down, and new life emerged—life full of hope and promise.

Through that time of testing and growing my roots deep, I learned some crucial strategies to stand firm and hold my ground when the enemy came around intimidating me, whispering lies, and enticing me to doubt the love and truth of Jesus and my Heavenly Father; he will do the same to you. Remember, the devil comes only to steal, kill, and destroy (John 10:10). He is angry that he has lost ground in your life, and he will try to gain it back. He does not want you walking in your destiny and purpose for which God has called you. He knows that as you walk into freedom, you become a threat to him, for you are no longer his victim. You are a victor who has overcome—a victor who can help set others free.

Consider this chapter your Healing Maintenance Plan where you will learn key strategies to help you grow deeper in His love and protect your healing progress. You will learn the importance of (1) focusing on Jesus, (2) filling up to overflowing, and (3) fortifying your mind and heart.

The three parts of the maintenance plan work together to keep you and your identity firm in Jesus' love for you. Imagine a three-legged stool. When the three legs are of equal length and positioned correctly, the stool is balanced and stable. You can firmly stand or sit on it without falling over. My prayer is that these strategies will deepen your relationship with Jesus and help grow your roots deep, deep, deep in His love and truth. When you are in Christ, you have the ability and strength to stand firm and hold your ground. You have Jesus by your side and the power of the Holy Spirit within you. When you are weak, He is strong. When the winds buffet you and threaten to blow you over, stand firm, for greater is He who is in you than he who is in the world (1 John 4:4).

FOCUS on Jesus.

One of the first lessons Jesus taught me was to keep my eyes on Him. What you and I set our eyes upon becomes our focus. What becomes our focus occupies our minds. What occupies our minds drives our thoughts, and our thoughts can easily pull us into a whirlwind of anxiousness or the calm waters of peace. We have the ability to choose upon that which we are going to focus. Choose each day to keep your eyes on Jesus—the way, the truth, and the life (John 14:6).

During times of "reacting" instead of "responding," turn your focus to Jesus unashamedly; do not pretend the situation is not happening. Do not run from Him and hide; run to Him and ask for help. Remember, the devil's goal is to drive you away from Jesus. He wants to isolate you, whisper lies, and beat you up.

The safest place you can be is with Jesus.

As you consciously turn your focus to Jesus, bring all with which you are struggling to Him. That is what Jesus longs for you to do. He does not want, nor expect, you to figure out everything on your own. Do not believe satan's lie that "You're too needy." Jesus sees you as His beloved who is worth each moment of His time. Through the Holy Spirit, He is always available to you.

Do not believe satan's lie that "Jesus is impatient with you or upset that you don't have it all together yet." Jesus came to be your Healer and Helper; His grace is all-sufficient.

Do not believe the lie satan whispers that "Jesus is keeping track of all your wrongs." Jesus is not a taskmaster keeping a list of all the times you messed up or got it right. He is a relationship-builder set on encouraging you and doing life with you. His mercies are new every morning.

Do not believe satan's lie that "Jesus is too busy for you." Jesus' desire is for you to be close to Him in an abiding relationship where you are safe to share your heart, your joys, your cares, your sorrows, your problems, even your anxious thoughts. When you are close to Jesus, sharing everything with

Him and focused on His love for you, the enemy cannot play his shame and blame game on you.

When tuned into the voice of Jesus, satan and his lies are tuned out.

When you catch yourself focusing on problems, worries, or falling into one of the enemy's snares, quickly turn your focus back to the One who is gazing back at you in love.

> *Cast all your anxieties on him, for he cares for you*
> *(1 Peter 5:7).*

FILL UP to overflowing.

As Jesus took my pain and toxic emotions and replaced them with His love and peace, I began to notice that He never left a void. When I asked Jesus about it, He shared that a void creates a vacuum, and a vacuum draws other things into it. He wants to fill us completely leaving no space for lies, fear, or anxiousness to get sucked back in. He wants us walking in the fullness of who He is and what He has for us. He wants every area in our life to become firmly rooted and established in His perfect love—His perfect love that casts out fear.

That made sense to me, and I began to pray a daily prayer, "Lord, fill me, fulfill me, overflow me, rest upon me, and swirl around me." At first, I was not sure why I was praying those exact words, but I was coming to trust that as words flowed from me in prayer, that it was the Holy Spirit directing me how to pray. I wanted to be filled up to overflowing with His love and power. I wanted His Presence resting upon me and flowing through me so I could change the atmosphere around me. One day as I was reading in Ephesians, I saw my prayer in the following verses.

> *And I pray that you, being rooted and established in love, may*
> *have power, together with all the Lord's holy people, to grasp*
> *how wide and long and high and deep is the love of Christ,*

*and to know this love that surpasses knowledge—that you may
be filled to the measure of the fullness of God
(Ephesians 3:17-19).*

Other verses in Colossians captured my attention.

*For God was pleased to have all the fullness of God dwell in
Him (Jesus) and through Him (Jesus) reconcile to himself all
things, whether things on earth or things in heaven, by making
peace through His blood, shed on the cross (Colossians 1:19;
emphasis added).*

*For in Christ all the fullness of the Deity lives in bodily form,
and in Christ you have been brought to fullness. He is the head
over every power and authority (Colossians 2:9-10).*

Here are a few keys to help you fill-up to overflowing.

Key 1: Praise and Worship

Created for love, we are designed to respond to our Heavenly Father's
love. When we experience His love and are attuned to Him where we feel safe,
cared for, heard, and seen, we can open our hearts to receive His love and give
back our love and praise to Him. It is a circle of love. He loves us first, we
praise Him, He inhabits our praise, and pours out more of His love into our
hearts (1 John 4:19, Psalm 22:3). We not only give our worship and praise
where it is due, but we also get a benefit in the process!

When we turn our focus to our loving Heavenly Father and praise
Him, our focus shifts from fear and problems to our Source of love, help, and
answers. When I praise my Heavenly Father, I want my worship to be a love
song to Him. A song of thankfulness and gratitude for the song He continually sings over me (Zephaniah 3:17). May His love pour out on you today in
greater measure to overflowing.

*Shout for joy to the Lord, all the earth. Worship the Lord
with gladness; come before him with joyful songs. Know that
the Lord is God. It is he who made us, and we are his; we
are his people, the sheep of his pasture. Enter his gates with*

thanksgiving and his courts with praise; give thanks to him and praise his name. For the Lord is good and his love endures forever; his faithfulness continues through all generations (Psalm 100).

Key 2: Gratitude

Studies show that when we are consciously grateful, we tend to be less depressed and happier in life. Putting gratitude into practice and writing letters of gratitude—to God, Jesus, or others—improves mental health for extended periods of time.[36] When you and I are busy praising and expressing gratitude, we do not have time to mull over negative experiences and get caught up in worry. Sharing that for which we are grateful can help us spiritually, mentally, and physically. It can strengthen our roots in Him and help us overflow with thankfulness.

Just as you received Christ Jesus as Lord, continue to live your lives in Him, rooted and built up in Him, strengthened in the faith as you were taught and overflowing with thankfulness (Colossians 2:6).

Key 3: Help Others

We are needy beings, and God knows that we need Him. He is a good Father who helps us, teaches us, and pours out His love on us so that we can pour it out and share it with others. When we are open to receive our Heavenly Father's love, we become conduits of His love and can love others as ourselves. From that place, we can love and help others in their time of need with grateful hearts. As we help others, something happens in our brains to reduce stress in ourselves.

God, a rewarder of deeds done in love, has created us so that when we give of ourselves and unselfishly provide support to others, we reap physical benefits that help improve our health and reduce our stress levels. When we help another, that person receives the support he or she needs, and we benefit on a neurobiological level by reducing activity in the stress-and-threat related regions of the brain during stressful experiences.[37] It is a win-win! While we are helping others, our focus is not on ourselves or our problems. Our focus is on

God's love and how we can be a conduit to meet the needs of another. As we help others, stress is relieved in us. With thankful hearts, we give out love and return love to our Heavenly Father who pours out more of His love. Helping someone else from His love is a beautiful way to be filled to overflowing.

> *To love Him (God) with all your heart, with all your understanding, and with all your strength, and to love your neighbor as yourself is more important than all burnt offerings and sacrifices (Mark 12:33; emphasis added).*

> *Remember the words of the Lord Jesus, how he himself said, "It is more blessed to give than to receive" (Acts 20:35).*

FORTIFY your mind.

> *Be alert and of sober mind. Your enemy the devil prowls around like a roaring lion looking for someone to devour (1 Peter 5:8).*

Satan is continually seeking ways to influence our minds and hearts through painful experiences as well as our own sin, shameful behaviors, and faulty beliefs. He wants us to have negative thoughts about God, ourselves, others, and the situations surrounding us. He knows that good thoughts bring us into a place of peace. He also knows that negative thoughts bring us into a place of unrest, triggering a cascade of stress chemicals and hormones that can cause short and long-term damage to our health. He knows the power of a word, and he will whisper lies trying to get us to take agreement with him. He will use painful experiences to persuade us to think that we are unworthy, unwanted, and of no value. Satan will try to get us to doubt the love of our Heavenly Father. He will tell us that we are powerless so we will think we have no hope.

While the enemy is bombarding us, we are having our own war of thoughts inside our minds. We replay events from the recent day or week, the way people treated us, what we should have done or said differently, and so on. As a worrisome thought drifts by, we grab onto it, letting our imaginations run wild thinking the worst. On top of our conscious inner thoughts, we have thoughts coming up that are tied to triggered-past experiences.

Whew, those are a lot of thoughts. A recent study suggests that a person has an average of 80,000 thoughts a day, 90% of those thoughts are the same thoughts as the day before, and 80% of those are negative.[38]

I have good news. To Jesus, you are not a statistic, and you have the Holy Spirit to help you with your thoughts. As you journey into healing and freedom, your old thought patterns are being undone, and new thought patterns based in truth are taking shape. As you spend more time in the Secret Place with Jesus, you are making good memories with new truths and new thoughts. As you consciously think more on good things, you will think fewer negative thoughts. As you set your mind on Heavenly things, you will think less like the world (Colossians 3:2). As you walk through your healing journey with Jesus, you are being transformed—in your heart and in your mind.

Do not conform to the pattern of this world, but be transformed by the renewing of your mind (Romans 12:2).

Here are some ways to strengthen and fortify your mind.

1. Take God at His Word. As you read the inspired written Word, the Bible, grab hold of its instructions and promises. Memorize them. Plaster them to the windows of your emotions. Plant them deep in your soul. (Psalm 1:2-3; Proverbs 4:13; John 17:17)

2. Get off the worry train. Take your thoughts captive and bring them to Jesus. Talk to Him about why you are having anxious thoughts. Ask Him if you have any lies or faulty beliefs attached to recurring negative thoughts and unhealthy behaviors. If there are, ask Him to reveal them, dig them up, and plant His truth. (2 Corinthians 10:5)

3. Choose your thoughts carefully. You can consciously think only about one thing at a time. Consciously choose to feed your mind healthy nourishment through praise, worship, Scripture, and thinking on that which is true, noble, right, pure, lovely, admirable, excellent and praiseworthy. (Philippians 4:8)

4. Revisit good memories. When you remember and think on experiences that brought you peace, happiness, and joy, you strengthen those memories, and your brain releases feel-good chemicals that reduce stress. (Psalm 77:11-12)

5. Ask God to guard your thoughts with His peace. The Bible tells us not to be anxious. In thankfulness, we can bring it all to our Heavenly Father, climb up in His lap, and tell Him what is troubling us knowing He cares. Scripture says that when we do that, He will give us peace that transcends our understanding. His peace can calm the storms—in our troubled thoughts and in our hearts. (Philippians 4:6-7)

FORTIFY your heart.

As you have walked down the path of healing with Jesus and invited Him into painful places, you have no doubt walked through trauma, offered forgiveness, dug up roots, and now have fresh seeds of truth taking hold. You have invested time, energy, and most likely an abundance of tears in the process. Depending on the depth of pain and healing, your heart may need time and space to heal. While your heart is healing and new behaviors and thought processes are being established, it is important to protect the work you and Jesus have done together.

> *Above all else, guard your heart, for everything you do flows from it (Proverbs 4:23).*

Here are five ways to safeguard your heart.

1. Treat your heart with care. Your heart is precious to Jesus. He would never throw your heart to the ground for others to trample. If people in your life continually mistreat and hurt your heart, ask Jesus how to set healthy boundaries, protecting you from further damage. If you are in a relationship that is abusive—physically, emotionally, sexually, or mentally—I encourage you to seek help in removing yourself from the unhealthy situations. (Matthew 7:6)

2. Keep short accounts. If you have experienced a lot of pain and trauma in your life, you may feel like the healing journey is going to be a long road. It may or may not, but you do not want to keep adding more toxic emotions nor do you want additional offenders taking up space in your heart. When the words or actions of others hurt you choose to forgive quickly and give the hurt and pain to Jesus. Ask Him to fill you with His love and peace. Also, show yourself the same grace you show others by keeping short accounts with yourself. When you make a mistake or hurt someone else, ask forgiveness, forgive yourself, and then take a swim in the pool of God's grace and love. (Colossians 3:13)

3. Guard your gates. One of the ways the enemy likes to sneak into hearts is through the gates of our eyes and ears. Guard what goes into your ears and what you see. *Is it life-giving? Will it taint the soil Jesus is cultivating in your heart? Will it bring forth good fruit? Does it bring peace or does it make you feel anxious?* When I am in a situation, and something goes into my gates that should not, I quickly ask Jesus to cleanse my physical and spiritual senses along with my heart. (Matthew 6:22-23; Psalm 119:37)

4. Cultivate your soil. In planting, you want to cultivate the soil to loosen the dirt to help the necessary nutrients, air, and water go deep so that the roots can gain access to them. Ask the Holy Spirit to cultivate the soil of your heart to keep your heart soft and receptive to the Word of God and His truths. (Mark 4:20)

5. Keep a heart connection. Time spent with Jesus is life-giving. You can share things with Him in the Secret Place and also in every-day life. Find personal ways to connect your hearts throughout the day. Go on a hike, talking to God about the nature around you. Write a letter to Jesus and journal what He replies. Write down what Jesus, Father God, and the Holy Spirit share with you, meditate on it, and treasure it. (Luke 2:19)

I pray that you will take this chapter to heart. You have been through too much and worked too hard to let the enemy steal your freshly-planted truth. When the enemy tries getting you to doubt God's love for you or doubt that you were healed review what you wrote in your Healing Journal Workbook. Remember how you felt when Jesus reframed a memory into a place of peace; by doing so, you will be strengthening your reframed memory, and the peace you felt when that memory was stored will once again flood your heart and soul. It is also a great time to strengthen your voice and boldly tell the enemy to "Get lost!"

Friend, you are braver than you realize. You are a courageous victor. Stand firm in Jesus and protect your healing progress. Continue working through the exercises and sections in your Healing Journal Workbook with Jesus. At the end of the year, look back and celebrate how far you and Jesus have journeyed together, in love.

> *Be on your guard, stand firm in the faith, be courageous; be strong. Do everything in love (1 Corinthians 16:13).*

Well, here we are—the end of the book, but I hope not the end of our journey. I pray that the information, exercises, and the healing stories shared encouraged and helped you as you bravely stepped onto your own journey of healing and freedom with Jesus.

Your testimony holds power, and I encourage you to share the beautiful work you and Jesus have accomplished together. What Jesus has done for you can inspire someone else to grab the outstretched, nail-scarred hand of Jesus and begin a life-changing journey of healing, restoration, and freedom.

ENDNOTES

Part I

Chapter 6: The Perfect Father

1 "May the grace of the Lord Jesus Christ, and the love of God, and the fellowship of the Holy Spirit be with you all" (2 Corinthians 13:14). Other references Colossians 2:9, 2 Corinthians 1:21-22

Chapter 10: Release of Dreams

2 *"There are different kinds of working, but in all of them and in everyone it is the same God at work. Now to each one the manifestation of the Spirit is given for the common good. To one there is given through the Spirit a message of wisdom, to another a message of knowledge by means of the same Spirit, to another faith by the same Spirit, to another gifts of healing by that one Spirit, to another miraculous powers, to another prophecy, to another distinguishing between spirits, to another speaking in different kinds of tongues, and to still another the interpretation of tongues. All these are the work of one and the same Spirit, and he distributes them to each one, just as he determines"* (1 Corinthians 12:6-11).

3 *"I pray that the eyes of your heart may be enlightened in order that you may know the hope to which he has called you, the riches of his glorious inheritance in his holy people..."* (Ephesians 1:18).

Chapter 12: The Root of Fear

4 Psychologist Kim Burgess, PhD, director of the Pediatric Psychology Center in Rockville, Maryland, points out that it is normal for four and five-year-olds who are just beginning to understand abstract concepts to have fears that are more complex; fears of things they can see and fear of things they imagine like the monster under the bed, someone in their room, and what might happen when Mom and Dad are not nearby. These ages are also the peak age for nightmares, and since preschoolers have a hard time distinguishing fact from fantasy, their bad dreams can feel terrifyingly real. Reshma Memon Yaqub. "Monsters Under the Bed: Understanding Kid Fears." *Parents Magazine*, Parents.com, 23 Feb. 2018, www.parents.com/kids/development/behavioral/understanding-kid-fears/.

5 Elle Kaplan. "Why Unleashing Your Inner Child Will Make You Insanely Creative, According to Science." The Mission Daily, Medium, 17 Oct. 2016, medium.com/the-mission/how-acting-like-a-5-year-old-will-make-you-insanely-creative-and-successful-according-to-science-a0ff48283a98.

Chapter 14: Bashing in the Face of Fear

6 *"Do not be anxious about anything, but in every situation, by prayer and petition, with thanksgiving, present your requests to God. And the peace of God, which transcends all understanding, will guard your hearts and your minds in Christ Jesus"* (Philippians 4:6-7).

Part II

Chapter 21: Attunement and the Secret Place

7 E. James Wilder PH.D., Anna Kang, John Loppnow, Sungshim Loppnow. *Joyful Journey Listening to Immanuel.* East Peoria: Life Model Works, 2015, 35.

8 Dr. Caroline Leaf. *The Gift in You: Discovering New Life Through Gifts Hidden in Your Mind.* Southlake: Improve, Ltd., 2009, 146.

9 Athena Staik, Ph.D. "How to Regulate Your Body's Fear or Love Response to Make Conscious Changes to Your Brain, Part 3." *Psych Central.com*, 8 Sept. 2011, blogs.psychcentral.com/relationships/2011/04/ conscious-attention-regulating-fear-or-loveresponses-and-focused-positive-changes-in-the-brain-part-3/.

Chapter 23: Wired for Peace

10 Dr. Karl Lehman. *Outsmarting Yourself: Catching Your Past Invading the Present and What to Do about it.* 2nd Ed. Libertyville: The Joy Books-A Division of Three Chords Ministries, Inc., 2014, 5-16.

11 Dr. Caroline Leaf. "S1 E5: How to Deal with Trauma, and Overcome Toxic Thoughts & Memories!" *YouTube*, Dr Caroline Leaf, 9 May 2018, www.youtube.com/ watch?v=iUSIEHfQmns&t=29s.

12 Dr. Caroline Leaf. "S1 E5: How to Deal with Trauma, and Overcome Toxic Thoughts & Memories!" *YouTube*, Dr Caroline Leaf, 9 May 2018, www.youtube.com/watch?v=iUSIEHfQmns&t=29s.

13 "The Conscious, Subconscious, And Unconscious Mind – How Does It All Work?" *The Mind Unleashed*, 6 Nov. 2014, themindunleashed.com/2014/03/conscious-subconsciousuncon-scious-mind-work.html.

14 Dr. Caroline Leaf. "S1 E5: How to Deal with Trauma, and Overcome Toxic Thoughts & Memories!" *YouTube*, Dr Caroline Leaf, 9 May 2018, www.youtube.com/watch?v=iUSIEHfQmns&t=29s.

15 Dr. Karl Lehman. *Outsmarting Yourself: Catching Your Past Invading the Present and What to Do about it.* 2nd Ed., Libertyville: The Joy Books-A Division of Three Chords Ministries, Inc., 2014, 356.

16 "Getting Triggered." 1in6, 1in6.org/get-information/topics/self-regulation-andaddictions/ getting-triggered/.

Chapter 24: Root Emotions of Love and Fear

17 Dr. Caroline Leaf. *The Gift in You: Discovering New Life Through Gifts Hidden in Your Mind.* Southlake: Improve, Ltd., 2009, 143-145.

18 Dr. Caroline Leaf. "Toxic Thoughts | Dr. Caroline Leaf." *Blog | The Mind Changes the Brain | Dr. Caroline Leaf*, drleaf.com/about/toxic-thoughts/.

19 Dr. Neil Neimark. "The Fight or Flight Response." *The Fight or Flight Response - NeilMD.com*, www.thebodysoulconnection.com/EducationCenter/fight.html.

20 "Chronic Stress Puts Your Health at Risk." *Mayo Clinic*, Mayo Foundation for Medical Education and Research, 21 Apr. 2016, www.mayoclinic.org/healthy-lifestyle/stressmanagement/in-depth/stress/art-20046037.

21 "Post-Traumatic Stress Disorder." *MedlinePlus*, U.S. National Library of Medicine, 4 June 2018, medlineplus.gov/posttraumaticstressdisorder.html.

22 "Post-Traumatic Stress Disorder (PTSD)." *Mayo Clinic*, Mayo Foundation for Medical Education and Research, 25 Oct. 2017, www.mayoclinic.org/diseases-conditions/posttraumatic-stress-disorder/symptoms-causes/syc-2035596

23 Dr. Neil Neimark. "The Fight or Flight Response." *The Fight or Flight Response - NeilMD.com*, www.thebodysoulconnection.com/EducationCenter/fight.html.

24 Dr. Karl Lehman. *Outsmarting Yourself: Catching Your Past Invading the Present and What to Do about it.* 2nd Ed., Libertyville: The Joy Books-A Division of Three Chords Ministries, Inc., 2014, 68.

25 Joe Dispenza. "The Waves of the Future." *Dr. Joe Dispenza: Change from the Inside Out*, Encephalon, LLC, 2009, drjoedispenza.com/index.php?page_id=the_waves_of_future.

Chapter 25: Joy in Freedom

26 Everett Worthington. "The New Science of Forgiveness." Greater Good, September 1, 2004, greatergood.berkeley.edu/article/item/the_new_science_of_forgiveness#gsc.tab=0.

27 Barbara Elliott. "Forgiveness Therapy: a Clinical Intervention for Chronic Disease." Journal of Religion and Health, U.S. National Library of Medicine, June 2011, www.ncbi.nlm.nih.gov/pubmed/20177785. View at https://docplayer.net/47994613-Forgiveness-therapy-a-clinical-intervention-for-chronic-disease.html.

Chapter 28: Walking Through Traumatic Memories with Jesus

28 Jim Banks. *The Effects of Trauma And How to Deal With It.* 2nd Ed., Campbellsville: House of Healing Ministries, 2012, 76-77, 178-179.

29 Dr. Jennifer Sweeton. "The 3 Parts of Your Brain Affected by Trauma." *Psych Central*, 11 July 2017, psychcentral.com/blog/the-3-parts-of-your-brain-affected-by-trauma/.

30 Amadi O. Ihunwo, Ph.D., Lackson H. Tembo, and Charles Dzamalala. "The Dynamics of Adult Neurogenesis in Human Hippocampus." Advances in Pediatrics., U.S. National Library of Medicine, Dec. 2016, www.ncbi.nlm.nih.gov/pmc/articles/PMC5270414/.

31 J. Douglas Bremner. "Traumatic Stress: Effects on the Brain." Advances in Pediatrics., U.S. National Library of Medicine, Dec. 2006, www.ncbi.nlm.nih.gov/pmc/articles/PMC3181836/.

32 "PTSD Statistics." PTSD United, PTSD UNITED INC., www.ptsdunited.org/ptsd-statistics-2/.

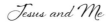

33 Sue Doucette. "Why Does Deep Breathing Calm You Down?" *LIVESTRONG.COM*, Leaf Group, 14 Aug. 2017, www.livestrong.com/article/136646-why-does-deep-breathing-calm-youdown/.

34 "STEP 4: Practice Your Breathing Skills." *Anxieties.com*, www.anxieties.com/57/panicstep4#. W1KTxNJKiUk.

35 "Grounded: Exercises in Trauma Therapy." *Greenwood Counseling Center*, 28 May 2018, greenwood-counselingcenter.com/grounded-exercises-in-trauma-therapy/.

Chapter 29: Protect Your Healing Progress

36 Joel Wong. "How Gratitude Changes You and Your Brain." *Greater Good*, Greater Good Science Center at UC Berkeley, 6 June 2017, greatergood.berkeley.edu/article/item/how_gratitude_changes_you_and_your_brain.

37 Christopher Bergland. "3 Specific Ways That Helping Others Benefits Your Brain." *Psychology Today*, Sussex Publishers, 21 Feb. 2016, www.psychologytoday.com/us/blog/the-athletes-way/201602/3-specific-ways-helpingothers-benefits-your-brain.

38 Maria Millett. "Challenge Your Negative Thoughts." *Challenge Your Negative Thoughts*, Michigan State University Extension, 31 Mar. 2017, msue.anr.msu.edu/news/challenge_your_negative_thoughts.